Print Publishing Guide

Adobe Press
San Jose, California

Print Publishing Guide

Adobe Press
San Jose, California

Library of Congress No.: 98-84553

ISBN: 1-56830-468-4

2000 99 98   4 3 2 First Printing: September 1998

The information in this book is furnished for informational use only, is subject to change without notice, and should not be construed as a commitment by Adobe Systems Incorporated. Adobe Systems Incorporated assumes no responsibility for any errors or inaccuracies that appear in this book. The software mentioned in this book is furnished under license and may only be used or copied in accordance with the terms of such license. Contact the software manufacturer directly for terms of software licenses for any software mentioned in this book not originating from Adobe Systems Incorporated.

PostScript® is a trademark of Adobe Systems Incorporated ("Adobe"), registered in the United States and elsewhere. PostScript can refer both to the PostScript language as specified by Adobe and to Adobe's implementation of its PostScript language interpreter.

Adobe, the Adobe Press logo, the Acrobat logo, FrameMaker, Illustrator, PageMaker, Photoshop, and PostScript are trademarks of Adobe Systems Incorporated. All other brand or product names are the trademarks or registered trademarks of their respective holders.

Published simultaneously in Canada.

Adobe Press books are published and distributed by Macmillan Computer Publishing USA. For information on current titles and individual purchases, visit www.adobe.com/adobepress or contact Macmillan at 1-800-428-5331 or 317-581-3500. For information, address Macmillan Computer Publishing USA, 201 West 103rd Street, Indianapolis, IN 46290. Macmillan's World Wide Web page URL is www.mcp.com.

This book was produced digitally by Macmillan Computer Publishing and manufactured using computer-to-plate technology (a film-less process) by GAC/Shepard Poorman, Indianapolis, Indiana.

autumn

Purpose & longevity separate an ordinary gadget from the invaluable tool.

MUCH LIKE A WELL APPOINTED KITCHEN,

A TOOL SHED IS FILLED SOLELY WITH

THE ESSENTIALS.

THOSE TOOLS THAT TURN TIRESOME CHORES

INTO A *JOY* & *TOOL* WITH

MAINTAIN CARE, WILL OUR PRODUCTS

PRUMING A LIFETIME OF USE.

boots

shovels

favorite essentials

tool shed   3

enhance the flavor of your meals with a

selection of herbs from Earth & Ware. While fall is usually reserved for

yard work and preparation for the colder months ahead,

it's also the perfect time to let her plants mature indoors.

During winter place them in a sunny kitchen window for a

convenient sprig or leaf of your favorite fresh herb. By spring you'll have

large, full plants ready to move outside.

organic herbs

spring seedling basket

fresh herbs   5

Contents

Introduction

Until recently, most prepress tasks—such as scanning color photographs, trapping, imposition, color correction, and half-tone screening—were performed exclusively by skilled specialists working manually or on expensive proprietary systems. Today many of these tasks can be accomplished on the desktop.

The flexibility and direct control offered by this new technology have blurred the traditional roles of designer and prepress professionals. Designers who have the knowledge and the equipment can do their own prepress work. The prepress industry has changed to support the new requirements of the desktop publisher. Many commercial print shops are equipped to transfer a designer's finished files onto film—a process referred to as *imaging* the files or *imagesetting*—and from film onto lithographic plates. Some shops can also image a file directly onto the plate without requiring film as an intermediary or even directly from a digital file to press. Some make recent developments such as high-fidelity color available to the desktop publisher. Prepress houses, as distinct from presses, provide a range of electronic prepress assistance that can include high-resolution scanning, color separation, and imagesetting.

Managing these changing relationships to achieve output of professional quality requires a knowledge of the processes and relevant issues. As a guide to the preparation of electronic files for commercial printing, this book addresses these issues, and supplies the information you will need in deciding whether to perform a particular task yourself or to leave that task in the hands of a prepress professional.

1

Color and Commercial Printing

Describing color

Print and prepress terms

Computer graphics

Image resolution and line screen

New print technology

Offset lithography

Other printing processes

Imposition and binding

Real-world project

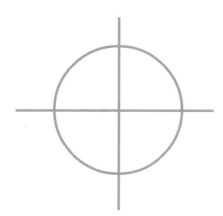

Color and Commercial Printing

One of the greatest challenges designers and publishers face is ensuring that the color in their printed artwork looks the way they intended. Accurate color reproduction requires a solid understanding of color basics and how color is displayed and printed on different devices, as well as good communication between the designer, the prepress service provider, and the commercial printer.

This chapter introduces fundamental printing concepts and terminology and describes several different printing processes.

Describing Color

Objects appear to be certain colors because of their ability to reflect, absorb, or transmit light, which we perceive as color. Our eyes are sensitive enough to perceive thousands of different colors in the spectrum of visible light—including many colors that cannot be displayed on a color monitor or printed on a commercial printing press.

We describe color in terms of three characteristics—hue, saturation, and brightness. These qualities are traditionally represented graphically on a *color wheel*. Brightness has to do with the sheer quantity of light reaching your eye—the brightness of a surface depends on how reflective it is. Hues depend on wavelength and are identified by color names. A hue corresponds to a direction on the color wheel. Saturation, also called chroma, refers to a color's vividness.

Two colors have the same hue and brightness but differ in saturation if one appears whiter or more neutral. Spectral colors, the colors of the single-wavelength light from a prism, have maximum saturation. The saturation of a pure spectral color can be reduced, while keeping the brightness steady, by dilution with white light. On a color wheel, which has spectral color along the rim, white at the center, and uniform brightness, saturation corresponds to distance from the center of the wheel.

Each type of device used to create a color publication—be it a scanner, color monitor, color desktop printer, or commercial printing press—reproduces a different range of color, or color *gamut*. Even similar devices, such as two monitors made by the same manufacturer, can show the same color differently. You can view many more colors on your monitor than you can print on a desktop printer or a commercial printing press. Varnishes and metallic inks can also create printed colors that cannot be represented on a monitor. In addition, scanners and color monitors can use different models to describe color from those used by desktop printers and commercial presses. As colors move from the computer screen to the printing press, they're converted from one color model to another, sometimes resulting in dramatic changes.

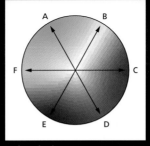

Color wheel
A. Green   B. Yellow   C. Red
D. Magenta   E. Blue   F. Cyan

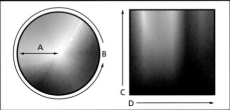

Color models

Designers can use different models to select and manipulate color, corresponding to the way color is generated in different media. On a television screen or computer monitor, a spot on the screen gives off varying amounts of red, green, and blue (RGB) light that combine to determine the spot's perceived color. When you manipulate color, using an image-editing program for example, you have the option of working in the RGB model and specifying colors by their red, green, and blue components.

The commercial color process uses four translucent inks: cyan, magenta, and yellow (CMY) together with a fourth ink (K), which is black. The black is used to deepen shadows and for printing type and lines. In the CMYK model you choose color by specifying ink densities. When you manipulate color using software, you have the option of working in either the RGB or the CMYK model, and you may decide to have images converted from one model to the other.

An image-editing program such as Adobe Photoshop provides other color model options besides RGB and CMYK. These include the hue, saturation, brightness (HSB) model, which lets you choose colors by the traditional color wheel method, and the Lab model, which uses the standard coordinates of colorimetry.

Red, green, and blue are called the additive primaries. If you combine 100% of red, green, and blue, you perceive white. If none of the additive primaries are present, you perceive black. Cyan, magenta, and yellow can be defined as the result of subtracting all the red, green, or blue from white. For example, if an object absorbs all the red light striking it and reflects green and blue, its color is cyan. If you combine 100% of cyan, magenta, and yellow, the result is complete absorption, or black. Cyan, magenta, and yellow are therefore called the subtractive primaries.

Color gamuts and color management

The range of colors a device can register or display is called its color *gamut*. The gamut of most output devices, including printers, is a fraction of the visible color spectrum. In addition, the color gamuts of different devices typically overlap but do not coincide. These differences often result in color appearing different in different contexts. To help ensure consistent color across output devices, software programs use color management systems. These systems tag files with color profiles of the relevant devices to ensure con-

sistent color through all stages of production. See page 62 for more information on color management.

Essentially by having a thumbnail sketch of the color gamut of each device in the workflow, a program that performs color management can link color expression at each stage of a print project—scanning, design, proofing, and production—and help the designer achieve reliable color in the final copy.

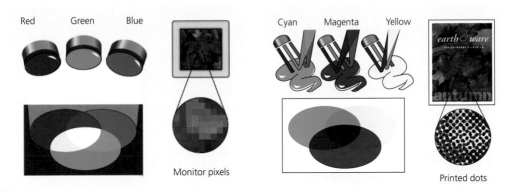

Additive color model: RGB   *Subtractive color model: CMY*

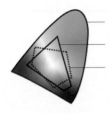

Visible spectrum
Display monitor (RGB)
Process colors (CMYK)

Visible spectrum and color gamuts

Print and Prepress Terms

Continuous-tone art and line art

Continuous-tone art is art, such as photographs, that consists of shades of gray and color gradations. Continuous-tone art is distinguished from line art, such as a wireframe drawing, which has no tonal variation. If you look closely at continuous-tone art, you will see that shades of gray or color blend smoothly without breaking up into dots. Once the art has been printed, the corresponding regions resolve under magnification into arrays of different-sized dots.

Halftone screens

Ink is an all-or-nothing medium in the sense that any given spot on the paper is either inked full strength or not at all. To simulate shades of gray or color on a commercial press, the image must be broken into arrays of dots of various sizes using *halftone screening*.

In the case of black-and-white photography, black dots are used to simulate shades of gray. Areas where the dots are small appear light gray, and areas where the dots are large appear dark gray or black.

To achieve a satisfactory range of color, the printer normally superimposes four arrays of dots—cyan, magenta, yellow, and black. A region with larger dots appears either more saturated with color or darker. The positioning, or *registration*, of the four arrays on top of each other can be critical.

Any visible pattern of interference between the four arrays can be distracting. To minimize the chance of interference, each array is oriented at a different angle on the page. If aligned at the correct angles, the dots form a field of rosettes. Looking for this pattern with a magnifying glass is one way of checking alignment.

Halftone screen with black ink

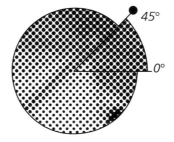

Halftone screens with process inks at different screen angles; correctly registered dots form rosettes

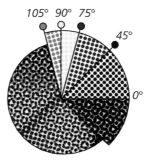

Spot colors and tints

Spot color refers to color printed using other than process inks. Each spot color is produced using a single ink and printing plate. You can choose from among hundreds of different spot-color inks.

Spot color may be used to reproduce colors not within the CMYK gamut. A spot color impression may also be used to "bump," or boost, the density of a process color. Spot color is also often used to save money when only one or two colors are needed since a job can then be printed on a less-expensive two-color printing press. See pages 56-58 for guidelines on choosing spot color.

A spot color printed at 100% density is a solid color and has no dot pattern. A tint is a lightened spot or process color created by printing smaller halftone dots. This process is typically referred to as *screening* by printers.

Process colors

In the four-color printing process, color is reproduced using three transparent pigments: cyan, magenta, and yellow (C, M, and Y). These are called process inks or colors. In theory, process colors create shades of gray when combined in equal combination and black when combined at full strength. Because of impurities in the actual inks, however, full-strength process inks create a muddy brown. To achieve contrast and detail in shadows, therefore, black ink is added to the process inks.

Using black ink to replace neutral combinations of C, M, and Y is also economical for printing and helps maintain the neutrality of midtones. Black is referred to as *the key* and is identified with the letter K.

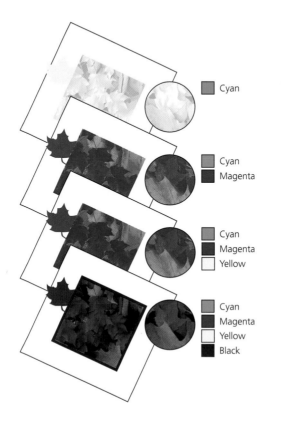

Cyan

Cyan
Magenta

Cyan
Magenta
Yellow

Cyan
Magenta
Yellow
Black

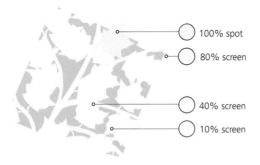

100% spot

80% screen

40% screen

10% screen

Separations

To print color art on a commercial press, each page is separated into component images called *separations*. Traditionally, separations have been created photographically using colored filters, with the results stored on pieces of film. Separations can also be created digitally, with the separations stored as files. There are at least four separations per page, one for each of the CMYK process colors and one for each spot color being used. Spot-color separations are sometimes called spot-color overlays.

If halftone screening is needed, each separation is screened separately to resolve it into an array of dots. This can be done either photographically or digitally. A commercial printer may require film separations to create plates for color printing, or may be prepared to print directly from digitally screened color separation files.

Undercolor removal and gray-component replacement

At any point on the page where the three CMY inks are being used at equal levels to produce a neutral gray, the combination can be replaced by black. To reduce redundancy and to avoid having too much ink on the page, printers use techniques of undercolor removal (UCR) and gray-component replacement (GCR). With UCR, black ink is used to deepen shadow and neutral (gray) areas in an image. With GCR, black ink replaces all neutral color areas.

GCR separations are generally considered easier to control on press than UCR separations. However, for images with a lot of detail in shadows, GCR may result in a flat, under-saturated look. In this case, printers recommend using UCR to add a small percentage of C, M, and Y inks back into the shadows. In Adobe Photoshop, the GCR setting gives you the ability to control the tonal areas that are replaced with black.

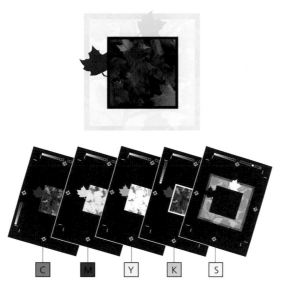

C   M   Y   K   S

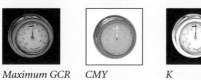

No GCR   CMY   K

Medium GCR   CMY   K

Maximum GCR   CMY   K

Knocking out and overprinting

Where artwork involves two objects or colored regions overlapping each other, a designer or printer can choose either to let the top object eliminate, or *knock-out*, what is beneath it or to allow *overprinting* as if the top object were partially transparent.

In most cases, you want an object to knock out the one below it so as to avoid unintended blends of color. However, overprinting can be used to create special effects or as a technique to hide flaws in registration.

Trapping

The quality of a printer's work depends on getting the different inks to print *in register*— that is, exactly aligned with each other. If one or more inks print out of register, white gaps may appear between adjacent objects where the paper shows through, or there may be fringes of unexpected color. To minimize the effects of misregistration, commercial printers developed trapping, a technique in which adjacent colors are allowed to overlap and slightly overprint along boundaries. Trapping can be done manually, in an illustration of an image-editing program, but today much of it is done by prepress software.

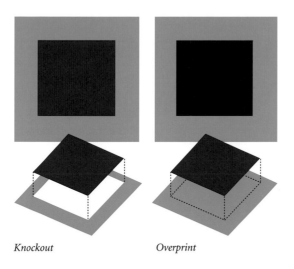

Knockout   *Overprint*

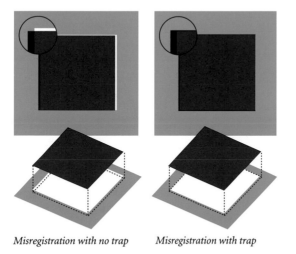

Misregistration with no trap   *Misregistration with trap*

Moiré patterns

When process-color separations are printed, the arrays of dots for each color are oriented at specific angles to minimize interference. For the best results, the screens are positioned so that the dots form a symmetrical pattern called a rosette, which the human eye merges into continuous-tone color.

If the arrays are poorly oriented, or if the paper shifts as it passes through the printing press, the rosette pattern may not print correctly. Instead, a noticeable pattern of interference lines, called a moiré pattern, may appear.

Misregistration

Paper sometimes stretches and shifts as it absorbs moisture and is pulled through a press. Printing plates can also stretch or be misaligned. These factors can cause multicolor jobs to print out of register, resulting in slight gaps or hue shifts between adjacent colors. Trapping and overprinting can conceal some of these flaws. Misregistration can also cause images to appear blurred or out of focus.

Dot gain

Many variables—from the photomechanical processes used to produce separations, to the paper type and press used—affect the size of printed dots. A certain amount of dot gain, or increase in halftone dot size, occurs naturally as wet ink spreads as it is absorbed by the paper. Dots may also increase in size as negatives from different sources are duplicated to produce the final film. If too much dot gain occurs, images and colors print darker or colors look more saturated than specified. See page 86 for more information on dot gain.

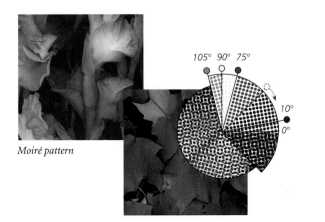

Moiré pattern

Registered   *Misregistered*

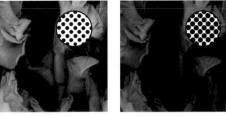

Halftone dots in a color proof   *Halftone dots after printing*

More Printing Terms

Device pixel. A device pixel is the smallest unit that an ouput device can display. A 300-dpi printer typically uses a 1/300" square device pixel; a 600-dpi printer uses a 1/600" square device pixel. Imagesetters, which are capable of much higher resolutions, can make a mark as small as a 1/3300" square dot. By comparison, most video monitors display with device pixels that are 1/72" square.

Device resolution (dpi). DPI refers to the resolution at which a device, such as your monitor or printer, can display text and graphics. Monitors are usually 100 dpi or less, laser printers are 300 dpi or more, and imagesetters are 1200 dpi or more. An image printed on an imagesetter looks sharper than the same image printed on a laser printer.

Image resolution (ppi). Image resolution is the number of pixels displayed per unit of length in an image, usually measured in pixels per inch. An image with a high resolution contains more, and therefore smaller, pixels than an image of the same dimensions with a low resolution. For best results, use an image resolution that is proportional to, but not the same as, printer resolution.

Line screen (lpi). Line screen, also called screen ruling or screen frequency, is the number of printer dots or halftone cells per inch used to print grayscale or color images. Line screen is measured in lines per inch (lpi)—or lines of cells per inch in a halftone screen.

PostScript. The PostScript language is a page description language developed by Adobe Systems as a way to exactly describe to a printer an image on a page. The introduction of PostScript printers revolutionized desktop publishing, and PostScript has become the standard way for a computer to communicate with a printer.

RIP (Raster Image Processor). The RIP performs the function of interpreting the PostScript code sent from an application and translating it to instructions for the marking engine that marks the pixels on the paper or film that is output. A RIP is built into all PostScript desktop printers and is a separate component for imagesetters. Some RIPs are also software-based.

PDF (Adobe Portable Document Format). PDF is a document format developed for handling documents in a device- and platform-independent manner. It allows files to be viewed, transmitted, printed, and archived in a single format. The PDF format works on all major systems, including Macintosh, Windows, and UNIX. Adobe Acrobat software provides for the conversion of documents into PDF, and lets documents be created in virtually any application and on any platform. When converted into PDF, documents retain a full range of color, graphics, and high-quality typography.

Computer Graphics

Vector graphics

The objects in vector graphics are made up of mathematically defined curves and line segments. You can edit the graphic by moving and resizing the entire graphic or selected components. Curves in vector graphics are determined by the points you select for the lines to pass through: You change the shape of a curve by dragging these control points.

Because the objects in them are defined mathematically, vector graphics take up comparatively little memory and are not tied to a particular display grid. When displayed or printed, the graphics are calculated to fit whatever screen or printer is used. The vector graphics are therefore considered *resolution-independent* and *scaleable*: Unlike raster images, they can easily be mapped onto different-sized screens or grids with different numbers of pixels.

Raster images

Raster images, also call bitmap images, are formed by a rectangular grid of small squares, or pixels. Each pixel contains data that describes its gray level or color tone. Raster images are apt to take up more room in storage than vector graphics do.

Because a raster image is made up of a fixed number of pixels, the resolution at which the image is output depends on its dimensions. A square raster that is 100 pixels wide, for example, will have a resolution of 100 pixels per inch if printed in an inch-wide square. If printed at twice the size, however, it will have half the resolution.

Unlike vector graphics, which are edited by altering lines and shapes, raster images are edited by manipulating groups of pixels. Because a raster image inhabits a particular grid, there can be problems associated with enlarging it or moving it to a grid with more pixels. In simple enlargement, the individual pixels are enlarged and may become visible as jagged lines. In transferring an image to a grid with more pixels, the colors or gray levels for the new pixels must be inferred by a process of interpolation that may cause blurring.

Vector graphics describe shapes mathematically.

Bitmap images describe shapes with pixels.

Image Resolution and Line Screen

Spatial resolution, typically some number of dots per inch, corresponds roughly to the ability to render graphic detail. On a computer screen, it's the number of pixels per linear inch (ppi); on an output device, it's the number of dots printed in a linear inch (dpi); on a scanner, it's the number of pixels sampled per linear inch of the scanned image. The resolution of a raster image depends on the size it is printed as well as on the pixel dimensions of the file. Pixel dimensions determine file size, and as a practical matter, file-size is related to storage and processing costs.

If you are having images scanned, you have control over the resolution and can choose whatever you think will produce the best results. If resolution is unnecessarily high, files will take a long time to display and image; if resolution is too low, the quality of output will suffer. The choice of resolution should be based on three factors: intended halftone screening lines per inch, subject matter, and intended screening method.

As a general rule, the scan resolution should be double the lines per inch you intend to use for halftone screening, although this can vary. With naturally textured images, such as long-range shots of water, foliage, and wildlife, you may produce good results with an image resolution that is one-and-a-half times or even equal to the screen frequency.

You may also be able to use lower resolutions with nontraditional forms of screening, such as stochastic or frequency modulation screening. Use high resolution where close-up detail is critical and where lines must be sharp, as with images of crystal and metal.

Image resolution: 72 ppi

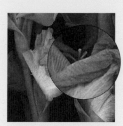

Image resolution: 300 ppi

Image resolution: 300 ppi
Output resolution: 300 dpi

Image resolution: 300 ppi
Output resolution: 2400 dpi

65 lpi: Coarse screen often used for newsletters and coupons.

85 lpi: Average screen often used for newspapers.

133 lpi: Fine screen often used for magazines.

177 lpi: Very fine screen often used for annual reports and art books.

New Print Technology

Frequency modulation screening

Traditional halftone screening arranges the dots in a regular grid pattern. Frequency modulation (FM) screening and stochastic screening both arrange dots in irregular crowds rather than in orderly formation. Screens made this way cannot have repeating patterns of interference and are therefore free from moiré.

Traditional halftone screening uses the size of the dot to modulate between gray levels: larger dots for darker shades, smaller dots for lighter shades. Frequency modulation screening controls the level of gray or color by varying how close the dots are to each other in the crowd. It distributes dots randomly but controls the number of dots in each area: more dots produce a darker area, fewer dots produce lighter areas. To use FM screening, you need special software or an imagesetter that supports it.

Besides its freedom from moiré, FM screening has other advantages over the traditional method. Because it uses smaller dots, printed images may display more detail and subtle gradations of color. On the other hand, colors that should appear solid may appear blotchy, and text and vector art may look fuzzy where they overlap screened colors.

High-fidelity color printing

Much research has gone into trying to expand the range of colors produced by process color printing. One of the solutions has been to print additional inks, such as R, G, and B inks, or green and orange inks. The addition of these inks produces a rich, saturated color gamut but presents challenges to the traditional screening process. Stochastic screening plays an important role in the success of high-fidelity color printing since it allows the additional inks to be printed without risk of moirés.

A commercial high-fidelity color system is the Pantone Hexachrome system. This system enables you to use up to six inks in combination to produce up to 90% of the Pantone spot color library.

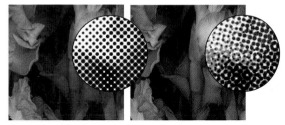

Conventional halftone screening

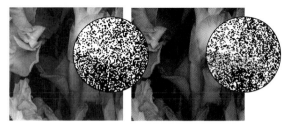

FM screening

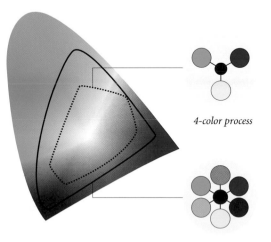

4-color process

7-color process

Color management with ICC Profiles

The ICC profile is a standardized format worked out by the International Color Consortium for describing the color behavior of any device. It is open for use by all manufacturers. Profiles can provide a thumbnail sketch of the color behavior of each device in the workflow, so that whatever program is performing color management can link color expression at each stage of a print project—scanning, design, proofing, and production.

The behavior of every color-handling device is based on its set of key reference colors. With a monitor, the key reference colors are the red, green, and blue of its phosphors—however, different monitors use different phosphors. With a scanner, the key reference colors are the colors of the filters on which the scanner's sensitivity to color depends—different scanners use different colored filters.

An ICC profile records the key reference colors of a device in standard colorimetric coordinates. When you get a file of scan data that has the scanner's ICC profile embedded in it, your computer can tell the scanner's key reference colors and can, in effect, reconstruct the colors that the scanner digitized.

To date, the most effective means of color management involves tagging each image file originating from a device with the ICC profile of that device. This makes the colors in the image accurately interpretable by any ICC-aware application.

Direct-digital printing

In direct-digital printing, presses are connected to workstations that create PostScript files from digital files, screen raster images, and send the files to the press. The presses do not require film or, in some cases, printing plates. Some direct-digital presses transfer digital information onto electrophotographic cylinders instead of plates and use toner to print four-color pages. Other presses send the digitized pages directly to special plates mounted on the press.

Direct-digital printing produces fast turnaround times, low production costs, and the ability to easily personalize publications. It is often used for on-demand or short-run color printing, where only a small number of copies are printed. It is not suited for high-volume, high-quality print jobs.

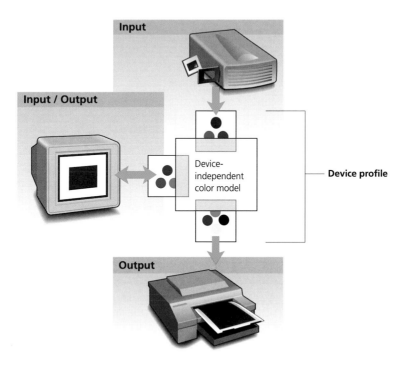

Input

Input / Output

Device-independent color model

Device profile

Output

Web-style direct-digital press

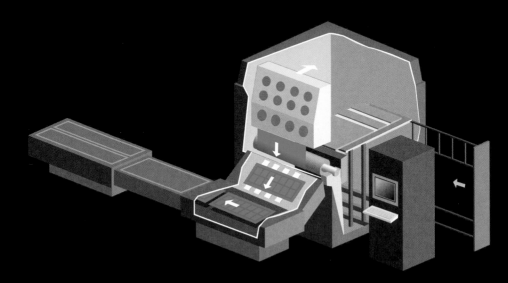

A computer-to-plate system accepts PostScript digital files and images them directly onto aluminum or polyester plates. The plates are loaded in sequence and carried to the printing engine where they wrap around a spinning drum along which the imaging head moves. The plates are then conveyed to a processor.

Computer-to-Plate Imagesetting

Computer-to-plate (CTP) imagesetters, also called direct-to-plate imagesetters, work like film imagesetters except that laser diodes image dots onto an aluminum or polyester surface rather than a piece of film. This eliminates a costly and time-consuming step on the way to press. CTP imagesetters also often produce higher print quality by avoiding multiple generations of film processing.

CTP imagesetters accept PostScript files and produce large format proofsheets digitally. Because digital proofs don't allow proofing of traps and changes are extremely costly, CTP imagesetting is best used when the publisher has full confidence that the files being handed off to the printer will not require changes.

Offset Lithography

You can choose from several different processes to print a publication: Flexography, gravure, screen printing, and offset lithography are the most common. The method you choose depends on your budget, your choice of a commercial printer, and the printed results you want. Because offset lithography is the most popular printing process, we use it here to explain the basics of commercial printing.

Unlike other types of printing, offset lithography involves printing from a flat surface. The printing plate holds ink because the image area is treated so that it is receptive to oil-based ink but not to water—not because the image area is raised (as in flexography) or etched (as in gravure).

A multicolor offset press has a separate printing unit for each ink being printed. If, for example, you're using process colors and one spot color in a print job and your commercial printer's press can handle five inks, a printing unit will be set up for each ink. The paper will then pass through each unit in succession. If the press handles fewer inks, your printer will print two or three inks first, stop the press and change the inks, and then run the paper through again to print the remaining inks.

Platemaking
Using a photographic process, a printer exposes the reversed image from the film separation (a negative) onto a flat plate with a light-sensitive coating, and then develops the plate. The image area of the plate—now a readable positive—is coated with a chemical that attracts ink but repels water. The non-image area is coated so that it attracts water and repels ink.

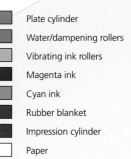

⬛	Plate cylinder
⬛	Water/dampening rollers
⬜	Vibrating ink rollers
⬛	Magenta ink
⬛	Cyan ink
⬛	Rubber blanket
⬛	Impression cylinder
⬜	Paper

A printing press repeats the wetting, inking, offsetting, and printing steps for each ink over and over throughout the print run.

   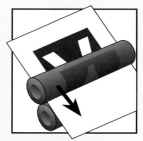

Wetting

The plate is mounted on a rotating cylinder. When the press starts, the plate comes into contact with water rollers first. Dampening solution (water plus additives) flows constantly from a traylike fountain through a series of rollers to the plate cylinder. The last water roller wets the entire printing plate, except where the plate has been treated to resist water.

Inking

Next, the ink roller applies oil-based ink to the plate. Thick, greasy ink flows from another fountain through a series of vibrating rollers, which distribute the ink thinly and evenly. When the last ink roller contacts the wet printing plate, it smoothly distributes ink across the water-resistant image area.

Offsetting

The final roller is a rubber blanket, which is pressed against the printing plate and carries away a reversed inked image (the offsetting step). The rubber blanket has some flexibility and gives slightly when pressed against paper, so the image can transfer evenly to both smooth and textured paper.

Printing

In the last step, the paper—in individual sheets (sheet-fed) or on a continuous roll (web-fed)—passes between the rubber blanket and an impression cylinder. The inked blanket cylinder with its reversed image presses against the paper, printing the positive image.

Other Printing Processes

Flexography

Flexography uses a raised-image plate made of flexible rubber or photopolymer that prints directly onto a surface. The flexible plate makes it possible to print on irregular surfaces such as coffee mugs, aluminum cans, or corrugated cardboard. Because of the soft plates, flexography involves higher dot gain and a greater risk of misregistration. Ink coverage is not as thorough and the screen ruling used cannot be as fine as with conventional lithography.

Gravure

Gravure printing uses an etched copper cylinder or wraparound plate where the surface of the cylinder represents the non-printing areas. The plate rotates in a bath of ink and the ink is retained in the etched wells of the plate. There are three types of gravure printing: conventional, variable area-variable depth, and direct transfer. Conventional gravure is often used for short-run, high-quality printing. Variable area-variable depth gravure is an excellent process for reproducing newspaper supplements, magazines, and mail-order catalogs. Dot gain can be lower than with offset. Direct transfer gravure is used mainly for packaging.

If you decide to use gravure, your film positives will need to be developed to different standards than for an offset press. The paper stock must be relatively smooth, since irregularities can cause the paper to miss contact with the tiny wells of ink.

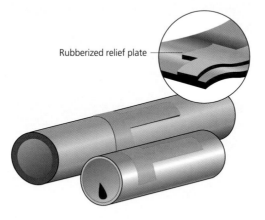

Rubberized relief plate

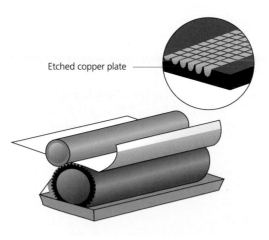

Etched copper plate

Screen printing

Screen printing, such as traditional "silk screening," is the relatively simple method of forcing ink through a screen stencil and onto a printable surface. It can be used to reproduce a few colors, or continuous-tone art. Because screen printing lays down the ink up to 30 times thicker than lithography, the color is more dense and durable than other printing processes. Commercial screen printing uses photographic stencils to transfer designs onto almost any printable surface, including posters, clothing, compact discs, and bottles.

Screen printing on fabrics may involve using larger traps to cover for misregistration. Dot gain may be unpredictable on fabrics whose absorbency varies. Synthetic fabrics will usually take a sharper image than natural fabrics. A relatively low screen ruling of 35-55 lines per inch is appropriate for fabric. The half-tone dots must be large enough to adhere to the mesh. One of the attractions of screen printing is the great variety of ink available, including glossy and florescent inks.

Thermography

Thermography is a finishing process that uses special non-drying inks on offset presses. After the ink is placed onto the printing surface, it is dusted with a powder. The surface then passes under a heater, which fuses the ink and the powdered compound causing these areas to swell. The printing swells or raises in relief to produce an engraved effect. This process is used to create business cards, stationery, invitations, and greeting cards.

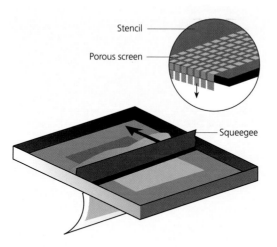

Stencil

Porous screen

Squeegee

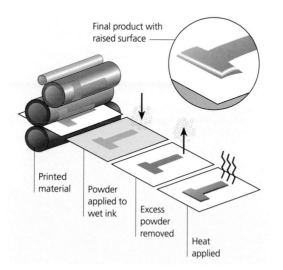

Final product with
raised surface

Printed
material

Powder
applied to
wet ink

Excess
powder
removed

Heat
applied

Imposition and Binding

Imposition is the process of arranging the pages of a publication so that when the sheets are printed and folded for binding, the pages will be in the proper sequence. Individual pages are arranged on a large sheet called a flat, which is used to produce plates for the printing process. Each plate prints a single form, or impression, of the imposed pages. Two forms are printed back to back on a press sheet that is folded into a signature. The signature is bound with others, if necessary, and trimmed to create a publication.

Imposition may be done manually or electronically. Manual imposition is a labor-intensive process where small pieces of film separations are precisely arranged and taped, or stripped, onto flats. Electronic imposition requires software that arranges the digital document into the proper formation.

Binding is the process of gathering folded signatures using one of several methods. In saddle-stitch binding, signatures are gathered to form a common spine and then stitched with staples. Perfect binding involves gathering groups of signatures, grinding the bound edge, and gluing the signatures at the spine into a one-piece paper cover.

When signatures are collated and folded for saddle-stitch binding, the inner pages may project outward slightly. The printed area moves slightly with respect to other pages. The more pages there are in a book, the farther out the pages closest to the center of the book move with respect to the other pages. This phenomenon is known as creep or shingling. If creep is not compensated for during imposition, graphics and text in a multiple-page publication will appear to move away from the gutter—where pages meet at the binding—in the first half of the book and toward the gutter in the second half of the book.

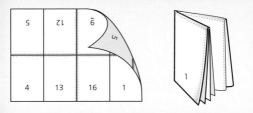

Imposed 16-page signature and folded signature

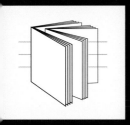

Inserted signatures

Saddle-stitch binding

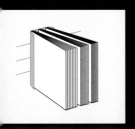

Gathered signatures

Perfect binding

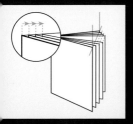

Creep occurs when the inner pages of a signature project outwards.

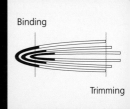

Binding

Trimming

Creep affects the printed area during binding and trimming.

As a first-time user of PageMaker, Mario Mirelez of Mirelez/Ross Incorporated created *The Art of the Garden* for an art exhibit at Eckert Fine Art in Indianapolis, Indiana. The limited edition of the exhibition catalog provided several creative challenges according to Mirelez, Director of Art & Design.

"First and foremost we wanted the catalog to be an effective sales brochure," Mirelez said, "both intelligent and legible. The piece was designed to feature the individual artists as well as their work. It was also designed to function not merely as a fine-art catalog, but to speak of the client's integrity as well."

The catalog was hand-collated, top-stitched five times, and bound with a spine protector glued to the cover. To give the catalog a more substantial feel, the front and back covers have gatefolds. As a finishing touch, a vellum overlay was printed and placed with the catalog, and they were bound with a foil stamp-embossed band.

At the end of each chapter of this book, we examine some of the key decisions Mirelez made while creating this award-winning publication.

"

Everything I've learned about printing:

Keep an open mind; stay proactive; pick

your battles; what you don't know learn;

it's okay if the printed piece looks better

than the proof; attitude is everything; and

finally, as with this quote, no matter

how much time you have to produce a

piece—it always comes down to the wire.

–Gina Long, Lithomania, Inc., San Francisco, CA

"

2

Constructing a Publication

Guidelines for specifying color

Using a color management system

Correcting color

Special printing techniques

Compensating for flaws in registration

Screen frequency, resolution, and gray levels

Compensating for dot gain

Scanning tips

Using duotones and tritones

Simplifying vector graphics

Image editing and interpolation

Scaling and resampling

Graphic file formats

Managing linked graphics

Using type

Choosing a font format

Real-world project

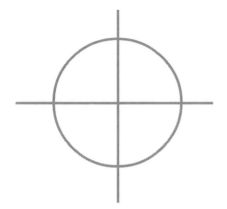

Constructing a Publication

The way you create your publication is not only critical to the success of your design—it affects the way your publication prints, both to an imagesetter and on a commercial press.

This chapter covers the issues involved in creating a digital publication for commercial printing, such as creating page layouts that avoid typical printing pitfalls, choosing the best graphic format, and compensating for misregistration using overprinting or trapping.

When properly assembled, a publication will print correctly and require less rework for you and your vendors.

Guidelines for Specifying Colors

You can specify colors either by referring to a color-matching system, traditionally the most reliable way, or by using a calibrated monitor. If you use one of the commercial color-matching systems, such as Pantone, TruMatch, or Focoltone, make sure your printer supports it. Color-matching systems are developed with rigorous specifications; printers who license a particular system agree to maintain the color standards specified by that system. If, instead, you specify colors on the monitor, your application or operating system should be performing color management.

When using an illustration program to create art that you will later carry over into your page-layout program, check that both support your preferred method for designating color. Naming the colors in your illustration exactly as you name them in your publication will save steps when you output your publication. To have colors match on the page, make sure colors are defined in the illustration program with the same component CMYK percentages as in your page-layout application.

Whether you use spot colors, process colors, or a combination of both in your publication depends on your budget, the purpose of the publication, the type of page elements you use, and how your design will be reproduced. A balanced approach to color printing helps ensure acceptable results. Use the following guidelines to determine what colors are suitable for your publication.

Use spot colors when

- You need one or two colors and you will not be reproducing process-color photographs.

- You want the effect of special inks, such as metallic, fluorescent, or pearlescent spot inks.

- You want to print logos or other graphics elements that require precise color matching or you're printing large areas of color throughout a publication and you want to ensure color consistency.

Use process colors when

- You need more than two colors in your publication. In general, printing with process inks costs less than printing with three or more spot inks.

- You want to reproduce scanned color photographs or color artwork that can only be reproduced with process colors.

Use spot and process colors together when

- Your requirements extend beyond ordinary process color. This could involve heightening color using a "bump" plate: a spot color plate serving to intensify one of the process colors. You should try to meet even high-end publication requirements with six inks—four process inks and two spot inks. Printing with more inks can be expensive because of the extra press work.

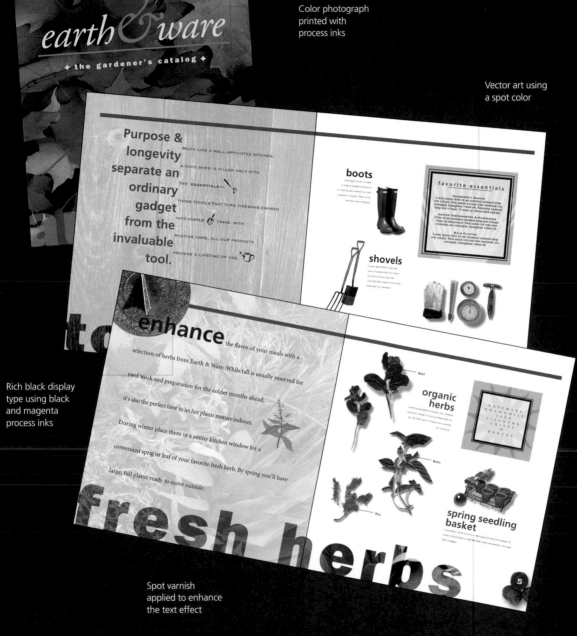

Color photograph
printed with
process inks

Vector art using
a spot color

Rich black display
type using black
and magenta
process inks

Spot varnish
applied to enhance
the text effect

Text with spot
color applied

Specifying Spot Colors and Varnishes

Specifying a spot color means that any page element assigned that color or any halftone tint of that color will appear on the same color separation. Name spot colors consistently across all the applications you are using, including illustration, raster image editing, and page-layout programs. The name you assign to a color does not determine what ink will be used in printing, but naming colors consistently helps ensure that your artwork will separate correctly and reduces the chance of confusion between you and your prepress service provider. You specify which spot ink should be used when you submit your files or film separations to the printer.

To save printing costs, if your artwork contains both spot and process colors you may decide to convert spot colors to their process-color equivalents so as to be able to print with fewer plates. When converting a spot color into a process color, be aware that many spot colors cannot be reproduced accurately with process inks. Use a spot color-to-process color conversion chart to determine the best process color alternative, or ask your printer for suggestions. If possible, print a test publication using the converted colors before the final printing.

Varnishes are used to protect a page, create a special effect, or accentuate photographs or display type. A flood varnish is applied to the entire area of the publication; a spot varnish is applied only to a specific area. As an alternative to varnish, many high-end presses use aqueous coating, which dries more quickly. In general, it's a good idea to use a varnish or aqueous coating on areas of a page with 100% or higher ink coverage.

Specify a spot varnish just as you would a spot color. Set spot varnishes as a spot color that will overprint and design a silhouette, or "mask," around the image or text to be coated. Adobe Photoshop provides for spot colors when it generates color separations, and has a mask feature applicable to silhouetting. Adobe Illustrator can also serve to create silhouettes for spot varnish. Consult your vendors to determine their requirements for specifying a varnish.

Spot color

*Spot color converted
to process*

Publication page

Varnish silhouette

50% screen

100% screen

Specifying Process Colors

To achieve predictable printed results, always use the CMYK values provided on printed color charts to specify process colors, or select colors from one of the process-color libraries.

Because process black is translucent and printing presses cannot lay large areas of solid ink smoothly, the addition of another process color to black is often beneficial. *Rich black* combines process black ink with one or more of the other process inks to achieve a more intense black. Use a rich black in areas where objects would show through process black and cause it to appear inconsistent.

Use a single, solid ink (such as 100% black or a dark spot color) to print hairline rules and small text. Fine elements printed with two or more colors are difficult to print in register, and misregistration can make the fine elements appear fuzzy.

Avoid creating process colors with high ink contents. Most printers recommend a maximum ink coverage of 250%-320%, so that the paper doesn't become oversaturated and stretch, warp, wrinkle, or tear. Oversaturation also increases the likelihood of misregistration.

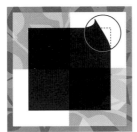

Process black (100% K)

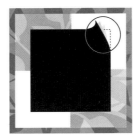

Neutral rich black created with 100% K + 20% C + 20% M + 20% Y

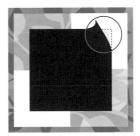

Cool rich black created with 100% K + 20% C

Warm rich black created with 100% K + 20% M

Process colors in small type and fine elements are more likely to show misregistration.

Black or spot colors in small type and fine elements produce a sharp edge.

Using a Color Management System

A color management system (CMS) is used to achieve color consistency between different devices. Ideally, this means that the colors on your monitor accurately represent both the colors in the scanned image and the colors you will see in your publication when it's printed. In fact, if a reliable, system-wide CMS is in use, you can achieve accurate color matching through all stages of the production process and in multiple contexts, including Web publications, composite color proofs, and final printed pieces.

Color management relies on an industry-standard color format developed by the International Color Consortium (ICC). With color management, a software application saves color files with ICC descriptions, called color profiles, of the applicable output devices. The application likewise reads in ICC profiles when it opens a color file. Photoshop, Illustrator, and PageMaker all support color management to help ensure consistent color as files move between these applications.

For color management to work effectively, all applications you use to process a color file must support color management, and ICC profiles must be selected for all output devices you will use. If you plan to choose colors on your monitor, the monitor must be calibrated and have an ICC profile selected. If your prepress service provider uses CMS, be sure to discuss the best way to ensure your project is compatible with their system.

"

The 'Digital Age' has empowered designers

to create their own images,

set their own type, and even make their

own traps. It also makes us more liable for

potential printing errors than ever before.

Knowing your tools and how

to use them has never been more essential.

—Clifford Stoltze, Stoltze Design, Boston, MA

"

Correcting Color

It may be necessary to correct the color in a scanned image, for several reasons. The original photograph may have a color cast caused by using incorrect film or lighting. Or the scan may have been imperfect—scanners can introduce color casts or artifacts. Or the colors in your original art may be out of gamut for the printing process and you may want to modify a color in the original to make it printable.

If using high-end scanned images, you can sometimes avoid the need to correct color later if you discuss your requirements with the scanner operator. A color cast in the original can be eliminated by a skilled scanner operator who knows what you want.

Using the histogram

Your image-editing program can be expected to provide a brightness histogram for the image you are editing. A histogram shows the number of pixels at each brightness level. A narrow histogram shows the image has a narrow tonal range. A broad histogram is usually desirable: one that is not too concentrated at either the dark end or the light end. You can force immediate changes in the histogram by adjusting brightness and contrast.

The choice of color mode

Color can be corrected in either RGB or CMYK mode. For a variety of reasons, it is often advisable to do most of the work in

RGB and then convert to CMYK for fine-tuning at the end. Whichever mode you work in, avoid unnecessary conversion back and forth. Repeated conversion allows small errors to build up and eventually may compromise the color quality.

Working in RGB mode

Typical desktop scans are in RGB mode and will probably require some color correction. Many experts believe it is best to do corrections and editing in RGB mode before converting to CMYK, for the following reasons:

- RGB files are smaller than CMYK files. Because there are only three channels of information in RGB files, rather than four as in CMYK, RGB files are smaller. Overall, work is usually faster in RGB.

- Some tools and functions perform better in RGB mode. Certain color-correction functions (Hue/Saturation, for instance) are more accurate in RGB mode than in CMYK mode.

- RGB gives you flexibility in how you use the image after color is corrected. For example, the image might appear in a newspaper ad, a high-quality brochure, a poster printed using European-standard inks, or it might end up on the Web. By working in RGB mode, you can apply a variety of Preferences settings to the same image, one for each printing device.

Average key image: Before correction, pixels are concentrated in midtones.

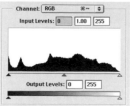

After correction, pixels are concentrated more evenly across highlights, midtones, and shadows.

Steps for Correcting Color

1. Make sure your system is calibrated and that your preferences are set for your printing environment.

2. Open the image in your image-editing program.

3. Decide which color mode to work in.

4. Save a backup copy of the original and resize if necessary.

5. Look at the histogram and notice overall features of the tonal range. Is the range too narrow? Is the image too dark or light?

6. Adjust brightness levels for a satisfactory tonal range.

7. Inspect individual colors and apply correction as needed.

8. Sharpen the image.

9. Convert the RGB image to CMYK if it is not already a CMYK file.

10. If necessary, fine-tune the image in CMYK mode.

Each time you adjust color in Adobe Photoshop, the color data in your file is permanently altered. Thus, your goal during correction and editing should be to perform as few adjustments as you need to achieve the results you want. Overediting and overcorrection may result in a degradation of pixel values.

Correcting Color *(continued)*

By comparison, color corrections in CMYK mode are device-specific. Once you have finished correcting the color in CMYK, you are locked into using a particular printing device. Moving to a different printing environment essentially means converting back into RGB.

Working in CMYK mode

A CMYK scan is device-specific, that is, optimized for output to a particular device. This means that colors and tonal range have been clipped to fit those of the printing device. If you plan to only print to that specific device, such a scan can be the best choice. Assuming your prepress vendor understands your requirements, high-end CMYK scans shouldn't need much correction. If they do need correction, it is best done in CMYK mode.

Avoid switching modes if you don't need to. If you are starting with a CMYK scan, consider staying in that mode all the way through. If a particular job requires editing, such as changing the color of red wine to white, it doesn't make sense to convert to RGB to make the change and then reconvert to CMYK.

If you start with an RGB scan, and perform the major part of the job in RGB, you still have an opportunity to do some fine-tuning at the end in CMYK. Here are some modifications you might want to save until you have converted to CMYK because they are better performed in that mode:

- You can specify definite CMYK color values in CMYK mode. If you want 100% cyan, for example, you can be sure of getting it since color values may change slightly in the process of converting an image from the RGB-CMYK modes. If you need to specify very dark, saturated colors, do this in CMYK mode.

- You can produce better gradients in CMYK mode. To produce gradients for printed work, create them in the final output mode, which is CMYK. The results will be smoother than when you create them in RGB mode.

Correcting the color plates

These examples show common color balance problems in an image along with the Curves adjustment in Adobe Photoshop needed to correct the problem. You can also use the color wheel to help you identify the cause of a color problem. For example, too much red in an image may be caused by too much magenta (as shown in the third example in the second row) or it may be caused by too little of red's opposing color on the color wheel, cyan (as shown in the second example in the second row). Similarly, a green cast is often a sign of too little magenta. Use this page and the color wheel on page 17 to help evaluate the color in your own image.

Corrected image

Heavy in black

Weak in black

Heavy in cyan

Weak in cyan

Heavy in magenta

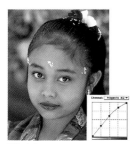

Weak in magenta

Heavy in yellow

Weak in yellow

Special Printing Techniques

Bleeds

Printing an object to the edge of the final printed piece requires creating a bleed. A bleed extends objects off the print area to ensure that when the printed paper is trimmed during the finishing process, the ink coverage extends to the edge of the paper.

Constructing bleeds requires that you focus on creating art from the perspective of the commercial printer. The accuracy of the press and the trimming equipment determine the size of your bleeds. When creating bleeds, avoid aligning objects exactly with the edge of the page. Pages are not always precisely trimmed at the trim marks.

You can extend most objects off the page to any size bleed. Consult your printer to determine the optimum bleed size for your job.

Bleeds extend to the edge of the paper.

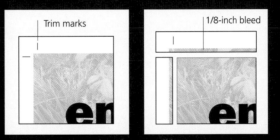

Trim marks indicate where the page will be cut.

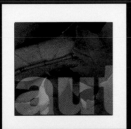

Avoid aligning objects exactly with the edge of the page.

Adjust the design so trimming looks intentional.

Crossovers

A crossover is a printed object that extends from one page to the next. Because a single object is printed on two sheets of paper, the pages must be carefully aligned in the final printed piece.

Binding methods affect crossover position and alignment. An object that spans the gutter may seem to disappear when the pages are bound, so you need to adjust the design accordingly. Also, when pages are gathered together for binding, some of the pages can be pushed out slightly. This phenomenon, called creep, can cause gaps or misalignment between the two parts of the crossover. Perfect-bound publications usually have less crossover misalignment than saddle-stitch publications. The center spread of a saddle-stitch publication will be exactly aligned because the two pages are printed on the same form, but adjacent pages closer to the cover may be misaligned. Follow these simple rules when creating a crossover:

- Avoid putting small text across two pages. Type becomes less legible as it approaches the gutter.

- Avoid using thin rules in crossovers; they are very difficult to align.

- Positioning a crossover in your publication is important, especially when the art is placed at an angle across the gutter. Diagonal crossovers exaggerate misalignment.

- Consult your printer about imposing the two pages onto the same form so that the color and ink coverage will be consistent for both pages. Printing pages on different forms can increase variations in color spreads.

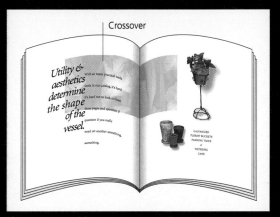

Crossovers extend from one page to another.

Before binding

After binding

Color shifts can occur when crossovers print on different forms.

Thicker rules help conceal misalignment.

Overprinting for Special Effects

Overprinting—blending inks printed on top of each other—can be used to create additional colors, special effects, and silhouettes. Typically, when you produce separations from a document with overlapping objects, the top objects replace, or *knock-out*, any colors beneath them on the other separations. In contrast, overprinting blends the background colors so that all of the inks for the overlapping objects print in the final piece.

Overprinting colors with uncommon inks combines the ink values in the overprinted color. For example, if a background color contains 50% C and the overprinted color has 60% M, the overprinted area will consist of 50% C and 60% M.

When you overprint colors with shared inks, common ink values are not combined. Instead, the ink values of the overprinted color are used in the printed color. For example, if a background color contains 50% C and 0% M and the overprinted color contains 20% C and 60% M, the printed color where the colors overlap will contain 20% C and 60% M.

Overprinting is also used to specify varnishes. Varnishes, which can be used to emphasize display text or to enhance images, can be treated like a clear spot color that is overprinted.

Because overprinting can increase the amount of ink coverage on the page and cause problems on the press, be sure to talk with your commercial printer before setting inks to overprint.

Overprinting can form a new color.

Overprinting can change the look of a color unexpectedly.

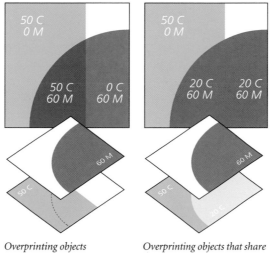

Overprinting objects without common inks combines the ink values where the objects overlap.

Overprinting objects that share inks reveals only the overprinted ink where the objects overlap.

Compensating for Flaws in Registration

When examining printed artwork, you'll often notice registration problems in areas where two colors meet. These are usually caused by the paper stretching or shifting slightly on the printing press. Where inks print out of register, gaps or color shifts can appear between the objects. Gaps are especially likely when adjacent objects share no common color and when objects knock out rather than overprint. Overprinting is often used as a way to neutralize the effects of misregistration. Another way of hiding flaws in registration is to slightly expand one region into another by adjoining a border strip called a stroke. This technique is called *trapping*.

Trapping

Effective trapping requires a thorough knowledge of color and design, and of when trapping is likely to be necessary. A publication designed with several interacting spot colors requires trapping because the colors do not share a common ink. A publication containing several process colors without common inks may also require trapping.

On the other hand, not all color publications require trapping. Designs that contain isolated areas of solid color don't need to be trapped because there are no adjacent colors that could show gaps if misregistration occurs. Designs composed of process colors where adjacent areas share sufficient percentages of component inks do not require trapping, since misregistration would reveal the common inks instead of leaving a gap. Four-color, continuous-tone images rarely need to be trapped because color changes are gradual and color is reproduced using semitransparent, overprinting inks.

An effective trap should compensate for misregistration without distorting the shapes of the objects on the page. If trapping results in distortion it may be preferable to protect against misregistration by overprinting. Overprinting thin black lines, small black text, and keylines can avoid the problem, even when these objects appear on a colored background. Illustrations that make extensive use of black outlines, such as cartoons or certain highly stylized art, may therefore require very little trapping.

Page designed to avoid trapping

Page requiring trapping

Chokes and spreads

A spread traps a light foreground object to a dark background. A choke traps a light background to a dark foreground object. Because the darker of two adjacent colors defines the visible edge of the object or text, spreading the lighter color slightly into the darker color maintains the visual edge.

A solid color object that overlaps both a lighter and darker background requires both spreads and chokes applied for effective trapping.

Trapping process colors

Process colors that share sufficient percentages of component inks don't require trapping because misregistration reveals a color that's similar to each of the adjacent colors. In the example shown here, the first two colors share sufficient percentages of common inks so that misregistration reveals a color that isn't visually distracting. However, the second two colors require trapping because they contain component ink percentages that differ enough to reveal a third color when the plates misregister. When adjacent colors each contain a significantly greater percentage of one component ink, a trap is usually required. Conversely, if all ink values in one color are greater than those in the other color, a trap is not necessary.

Rich blacks require a trapping technique called a keepaway. The undercolor—the process inks used to make a rich black—is made slightly smaller than the black area so that misregistration doesn't result in a tiny fringe of color. Should the inks misregister, the undercolor is covered by the black area. If you are using an image-editing program to produce rich blacks by undercolor addition (UCA), the option of automatic trapping may be available to prevent fringes. Photoshop, for example, offers automatic trapping for all CMYK images.

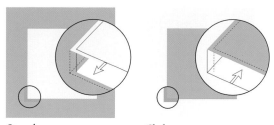

Spread *Choke*

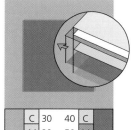

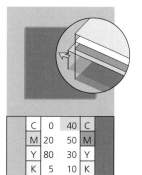

C	30	40	C
M	20	50	M
Y	10	30	Y
K	5	10	K

C	0	40	C
M	20	50	M
Y	80	30	Y
K	5	10	K

These colors share sufficient percentages of component inks, so poor registration reveals common inks.

These colors don't share sufficient percentages of component inks, so poor registration reveals a noticeable third color.

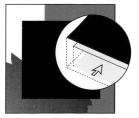
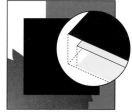

The undercolor of a rich black is pulled away from the edge…

so that when misregistration occurs, the undercolor will not show.

Overprinting to Cover Misregistration

In some situations, overprinting text and objects can be preferable to trapping as a way to hide misregistration. For example, small text and hairlines can be distorted by trapping. Overprinting preserves the shape of the object and the legibility of the text.

Before overprinting fine text and thin lines, evaluate whether misregistration will be more noticeable than a possible variation in the line or text color. Keep in mind that your solution should provide the least distraction between text (or line) and background should misregistration occur. Ask these questions to evaluate your situation:

- If gaps appear due to misregistration, will they be noticeable?

- Will the text change to an undesirable color if overprinted on the background?

- Will trapping distort the text characters?

Printing keylines around images is a common use of overprinting. The overprinted keyline can hide any misregistration that occurs when the image is printed. Ask your prepress service provider what keyline width to use.

Overprinted black text

Overprinted keyline

Black text set to knock-out, misregistered.

Black text set to overprint, misregistered.

Trapping Methods

Overprinting colors with shared inks

If objects share common ink colors, it is not necessary to trap the colors. In this case, the common ink hides slight areas of misregistration.

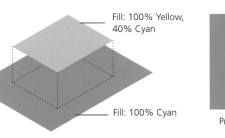

Fill: 100% Yellow, 40% Cyan

Fill: 100% Cyan

Printed result.
No trap or
overprint required.

Overprinting colors with no shared inks

If objects do not share common ink colors, use trap to add the overprint color to the background color where the two overlap.

Fill: 100% Magenta

Trap: 100% Magenta, 40% Cyan (Overprint)

Fill: 100% Cyan

Printed result.
Overprint stroke or trap:
100% Cyan,
100% Magenta

Trapping lines

Use when printing lines on a colored or black background.

Stroke:
1 pt. 100% Magenta

Stroke:
2 pt. 100% Magenta (Overprint)

Fill: 100% Cyan

Printed result.
.5 pt. trap

Black lines overprint (four-color black background)

Use when your illustration or type is reversed out of a four-color black background.

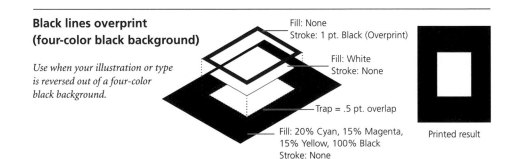

Fill: None
Stroke: 1 pt. Black (Overprint)

Fill: White
Stroke: None

Trap = .5 pt. overlap

Fill: 20% Cyan, 15% Magenta, 15% Yellow, 100% Black
Stroke: None

Printed result

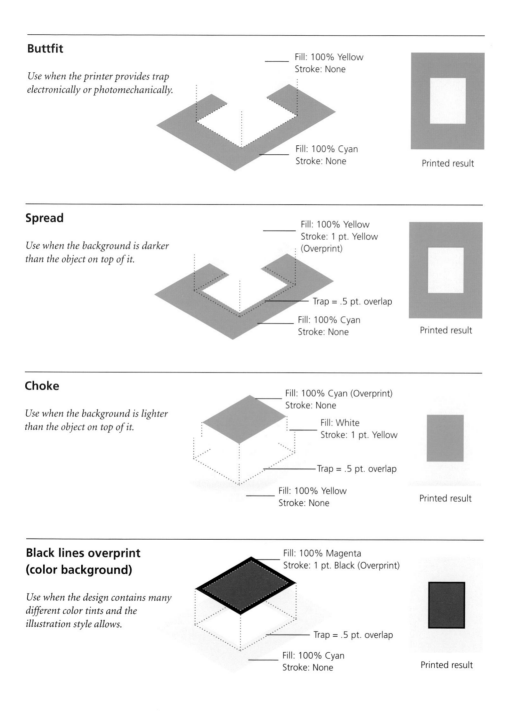

Buttfit

Use when the printer provides trap electronically or photomechanically.

Fill: 100% Yellow
Stroke: None

Fill: 100% Cyan
Stroke: None

Printed result

Spread

Use when the background is darker than the object on top of it.

Fill: 100% Yellow
Stroke: 1 pt. Yellow
(Overprint)

Trap = .5 pt. overlap

Fill: 100% Cyan
Stroke: None

Printed result

Choke

Use when the background is lighter than the object on top of it.

Fill: 100% Cyan (Overprint)
Stroke: None

Fill: White
Stroke: 1 pt. Yellow

Trap = .5 pt. overlap

Fill: 100% Yellow
Stroke: None

Printed result

Black lines overprint
(color background)

Use when the design contains many different color tints and the illustration style allows.

Fill: 100% Magenta
Stroke: 1 pt. Black (Overprint)

Trap = .5 pt. overlap

Fill: 100% Cyan
Stroke: None

Printed result

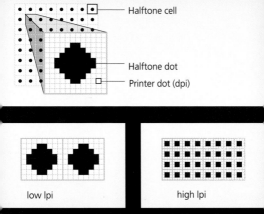

Halftone cell

Halftone dot

Printer dot (dpi)

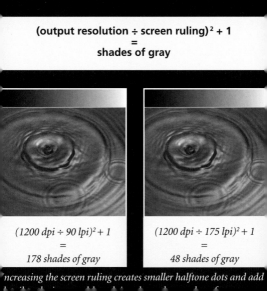

low lpi

high lpi

The lower the screen ruling, the larger the halftone cells; the higher the screen ruling, the smaller the halftone cells.

**(output resolution ÷ screen ruling)^2 + 1
=
shades of gray**

$(1200 \text{ dpi} ÷ 90 \text{ lpi})^2 + 1$
=
178 shades of gray

$(1200 \text{ dpi} ÷ 175 \text{ lpi})^2 + 1$
=
48 shades of gray

Increasing the screen ruling creates smaller halftone dots and add

Screen Frequency, Resolution, and Gray Levels

Screen frequency, also called screen ruling or halftone frequency, refers to the number of lines per inch (lpi) of halftone dots. The relationship between the imagesetter's resolution (dpi) and the screen ruling (lpi) determines the fineness or coarseness of the printed output. The same two factors also affect the number of gray levels or color tones available, measures of the *tonal depth* in the final image.

The screen ruling used to image film for a job depends on the resolution of the imagesetter and on the paper stock and type of press used to print the publication. A newspaper is commonly printed using a low screen ruling of 85 lpi because of newsprint's high absorbency of ink and the high speed of the press. A higher screen ruling would saturate the newsprint with ink and make the images look muddy. A four-color magazine printed on coated paper might use a screen ruling of 150-175 lpi, with art magazines using up to 200 lpi. Lower screen rulings make images appear coarse and less detailed.

Screen ruling also determines the size of a halftone cell, which in turn dictates the maximum size of a halftone dot. The halftone dot is made up of printer dots; printer resolution determines the number of dots available to create the halftone dot. The relationship between screen ruling and printer resolution determines the depth or tonal range that can

be printed. As the screen ruling increases, the size of the halftone cell decreases; fewer printer dots are used to create the halftone dot, so fewer gradations can be represented and the image may lose depth.

To calculate how many levels of gray are available at a particular screen ruling and output resolution, use the formula shown on the facing page. The maximum number of grays that most output devices can produce is 256. The levels of gray available also influence the smoothness of blends and gradients.

FINAL IMAGESETTER RESOLUTION	MAXIMUM LINE SCREEN FOR 256 GRAYS
300	19
400	25
600	38
900	56
1000	63
1270	79
1446	90
1524	95
1693	106
2000	125
2400	150
2540	159
3000	188
3252	203
3600	225
4000	250

Compensating for Dot Gain

Continuous-tone images are reproduced with halftone dots of different sizes—large dots reproduce dark tones and small dots reproduce light tones. During the reproduction process, the dots change in size, usually getting larger. This phenomenon is called dot gain. Printed images appear dark and dense unless you compensate for dot gain.

There are many sources of dot gain. Dot gain can occur during platemaking or when the inked plate transfers the image to the rubber blanket on press. The greatest gain, however, occurs when the dot lands on paper—the pressure of the press forces ink into the absorbent paper, which causes the inked halftone dots to spread.

The degree of overall dot gain for a particular press run depends on the printing environment. Individual dot gain depends primarily on the size of the dot. The midtone (50%) dot has the longest perimeter, and so it increases the most. Small highlight dots grow very little, and since large shadow dots overlap one another, they also show little gain. The accompanying graph shows the typical dot gain from film stage to press-sheet stage plotted against the percentage dot value (representing tone) found on the film. The curve peaks at the 50% tonal value and reaches zero at either end.

Halftone-dot percentages are measured with a densitometer—an instrument for measuring the relative density of any part of an image. A dot-gain percentage value refers to what happens to midtone dots. A 20% midtone dot gain, for instance, means that a 50% midtone dot will print on paper as a 70% dot. The quoted addition does not apply across the board to all sizes—as the graph illustrates, dots that are smaller or larger than midtone will have fewer percentage points added. In a process that expands 50% midtone dots into 70% dots, the 70% kind will only grow into ones that are about 85%. Larger dots are augmented by less than the full twenty points, in this case by only about fifteen points, and the same is true for those smaller than midtone as well.

Data on dot gain are published in the form of Specifications for Web-Offset Publication (SWOP) standards. These show a typical dot gain of 18-25% when printing on coated stock. It can be as low as 10% depending on the type of press, paper, and other factors. The data derive from a survey of U.S. printers and refer to midtone dot gain in going from film to printed paper. The facing illustrations show, in a magnified section of the same image, the typical dot gain when printing on coated stock, uncoated stock, and newsprint.

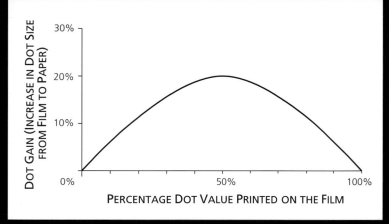

Typical dot gain throughout the tonal range (coated paper stock)

Dot gain on coated stock

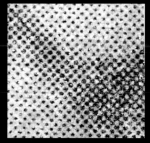

Dot gain on uncoated stock

Dot gain on newsprint

Paper Quality and Dot Gain

Paper quality is an important factor in determining your screen frequency. If the paper is porous, dot gain will obviate any detail that could be gained from using a high screen frequency. Papers and coatings come in a large variety of types and are intended for many different purposes.

Newsprint. A coarser paper made mostly from wood pulp and highly porous. It is manufactured almost exclusively for printing newspapers. The dot gain for newsprint can be as high as 30%, or more.

Uncoated Paper. Any number of different types of unvarnished paper. Dot gain for uncoated paper is roughly 20%. Expect a few percent variation either way depending on how fast the press is run and how subject the press is to regular minor adjustment by the operator. In general, sheet-fed presses run more slowly than web-fed presses, which in some cases may facilitate control.

Coated Paper. Paper that has been given a varnish coat, helping to seal the paper and reduce dot gain. On a sheet-fed press, the dot gain on coated stock can be as low as 10%, although 15% is probably more typical. High-quality grayscale and four-color images are usually printed on coated stock.

Supercalendered Paper. Calendering freshly made paper is analogous to ironing cloth. It is a normal finishing step involving heat and pressure. Supercalendering is done for some papers in order to get a smoother, less porous surface. Supercalendered paper can be coated or uncoated. Uncoated supercalendered stock can have a dot gain approximately as low as ordinary coated stock.

The figures given here for dot gain are intended mainly to show the extent of variation. Ask the printer what to expect from a specific stock on any given press. Some other terms that may come up in discussing paper are *acid-free* and *aqueous coating*. Acid-free paper is of particular interest when printed material must not darken over time. Aqueous coatings are applied optionally after printing. Because it covers the ink, a coating can help prevent ink from rubbing off. Aqueous coating can be either glossy or matte.

Scanning Tips

If your original scan is faulty or contains too little detail, it may be impossible to correct adequately. Use the following guidelines to ensure the best scan possible:

- Calculate the required scan resolution in advance. Anticipate future needs for enlargement, which would require a higher resolution scan. You pay a penalty for unnecessarily high resolution in terms of scanner time and file overhead.

- If you are using a desktop scanner, be wary of sharpening, adjusting contrast, or correcting color during the scan. Adjustments can usually be made more effectively later using an image-editing program, which will let you see the effect of a change before you commit to it. Modifications made during scanning are difficult to reverse if you don't like the result.

- Try to position the original correctly in the scanner, so as to minimize the need for rotation later.

- Identify the key elements, or "selling points," of your image. If possible, tailor the scan so those areas reproduce optimally. For instance, if the scan is for a clothing catalog, get the clothing right even if it means compromising other aspects.

- If you employ a color management system, use scanners with ICC profiles in your system to record the colorspace used by the scanner.

- Save any relevant scanner settings in your image file. Information about settings can be useful later when files are screened and output to film.

- Don't scan text unless it's large display type. The results will be better if you create a fresh rendering of text. You can re-create text using any application that supports PostScript. Use an image-editor if you need special effects.

- When scanning, keep in mind that file size grows faster than scan resolution. Doubling the scan resolution means there are twice as many pixels both horizontally and vertically and thus four times as many overall. The file size of an image scanned at 200 ppi is four times greater than when it is scanned at 100 ppi.

Choosing a Scan Resolution

Use the following guidelines for choosing your scan resolution:

- Because black lines on a plain background tend to show jagged edges easily, line art should be scanned at high resolution. If you have room to store the large files resulting from such a scan, it may make sense to scan at the resolution of the output device, which could be as high as 1200 dpi.

- Continuous-tone images will normally be scanned at a slightly lower resolution than line art, in preparation for digital screening. If you are having images scanned in the expectation of screening them, you need to calculate the appropriate scanning resolution.

- If you plan to use normal halftone screening for images that will print at their original size, a conservative approach for calculating scanning resolution is to double the screen ruling you expect to use. For example, if the screen ruling will be 150 lpi, the desired scan resolutions would be 300 ppi. Keep in mind, however, that images scanned at high resolutions require more disk storage space than images scanned at low resolutions. See "Overscanning" on page 94 for more information.

- If you plan to resize the image, allow for this in your choice of scanning resolution. Measure the original image, decide on the size of the final printed image, and calculate the enlargement ratio of final size to original size. Factor in the anticipated enlargement ratio so that you scan at a proportionally higher resolution.

- It makes a difference whether your images will be screened using frequency modulation (FM) or traditional halftones. The resolution to use for FM screening varies according to the particular method used, but in general you want to produce an FM dot that is close to the minimum size that your printing press can print consistently.

$$\frac{\text{final image height}}{\text{original image height}} \times \frac{\text{screen}}{\text{ruling}} \times 2 = \frac{\text{desired image resolution}}{}$$

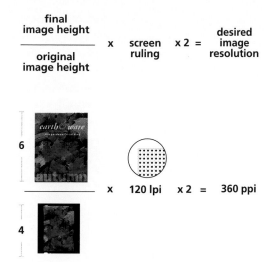

$$\frac{6}{4} \times 120 \text{ lpi} \times 2 = 360 \text{ ppi}$$

For images that will be resized, calculate the scaling factor and multiply it by twice the screen ruling.

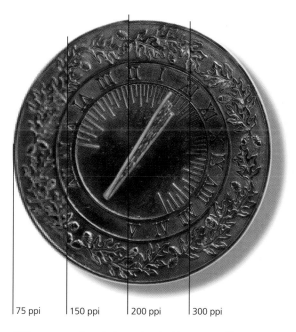

75 ppi   150 ppi   200 ppi   300 ppi

Different scanned resolutions printed with a screen ruling of 175 lpi.

Overscanning

Some images can be scanned at resolutions less than twice the output screen ruling. Images that do not contain geometric patterns, sharp edges, or straight lines can be scanned from 1.5 to 2 times the screen ruling. Fuzzy texture, foliage, and fur can often be scanned at even lower resolutions. In this example, despite one image having a larger file size and higher scanning resolution, the printed quality of the two images is the same. Scanning at a higher resolution produced a larger file without improving the quality of the final image. The image scanned at the lower resolution requires less disk space and takes less time to print.

Tips for working with scanned images

- Save your scanned image in TIFF format if you work on both the Macintosh and Windows platforms.

- To reduce imaging time, convert RGB images to CMYK images in an image-editing program before importing them into your page-layout application. If you use a color management system to make this conversion as accurate as possible, it should contain an ICC profile of the intended output device.

- If using high-end scanned images, make sure you discuss your expectations with the vendor before scanning begins. Most flaws in originals can be eliminated by a skilled scanner operator who knows what you want. Explain which elements need to be especially crisp or to match the original. Indicate if there are soft elements that should remain soft instead of being sharpened during the scan.

- To ensure good color reproduction early in the production process, you may wish to check color proofs of individual scanned images before they are placed in a page-layout program.

- Once a scanned image is taken into Photoshop, a histogram is available that shows the number of pixels at each brightness level. If the scan was under- or overexposed, the histogram will be unbalanced. If the image is too contrasty, the histogram will have too few pixels in the midrange. Gaps in the histogram can mean that not enough data was captured and that rescanning is necessary.

Scan resolution: 250 ppi
File size: 465K
Screen ruling: 133 lpi

Scan resolution: 400 ppi
File size: 1165K
Screen ruling: 133 lpi

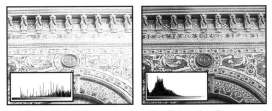

Original with insufficient detail, and sufficient detail

Original, and corrected high-key image

Original, and corrected low-key image

Using Duotones and Tritones

A single plate on a printing press can reproduce only about 50 levels of gray, substantially fewer than the range distinguishable in a good black-and-white photograph. Multitone printing with gray, or other non-black, inks has been used for years to enrich the tonal range when printing black-and-white photographs.

Duotones and tritones are grayscale images printed with two and three inks. The process resembles color separation printing except that the separate plates deliver black and one or more gray inks instead of various colors. Duotone and tritone printing can provide a dramatic improvement in the reproduction of subtle detail and in the overall quality of the image.

Duotone and tritone separation can be done digitally in an image-editing program such as Adobe Photoshop. This leaves it to the designer to decide how gray levels in the original should be translated into densities of the separate inks. To create a duotone digi-tally, the designer needs to specify two curves, one for each ink, that show how gray levels in the original are to be converted into ink density or halftone dot size. Some recommended curves are provided by the application, but the designer can also determine other curves by means of a Duotone Curve dialog box. For convenience, a curve can be specified by giving only two or three points along it and letting the program fill in the intermediate values.

To illustrate how varying the curves can change the appearance of a multitone image, the following pages show some examples of duotones, tritones, and quadtones created in Adobe Photoshop.The curves used to determine the distribution of each ink were created by specifying only three to six points on the curve. Although the dialog box lets you specify up to 13 points on the graph, you may specify a curve with far fewer. To print the results, Pantone black was used with various shades of gray.

A final consideration when creating duotones is that both the order in which the inks are printed and the screen angles you use have a dramatic effect on your final output. In general, to ensure the most fully saturated colors, darker inks should be printed before lighter inks. If you're using Photoshop to set the screen angles, use the Auto button in the Halftone Screens dialog box.

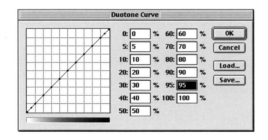

The Photoshop Duotone Curve dialog box allows you to specify the distribution of each ink by specifying density (i.e., dot size) adjustments for up to 13 points on the curve. The curve shown here is a linear curve, where each grayscale value from the original image is mapped to the same density value of the given ink.

Duotones

Printing Inks:

Ink 1:
Black

Ink 2:
PMS Cool Gray 10

Ink 1:
Black

0: **0** % 100: **95** %
50: **40** %

Ink 2:
PMS Cool Gray 10

0: **0.5** % 100: **70** %
50: **20** %

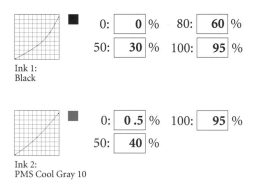

Ink 1:
Black

0: **0** % 80: **60** %
50: **30** % 100: **95** %

Ink 2:
PMS Cool Gray 10

0: **0.5** % 100: **95** %
50: **40** %

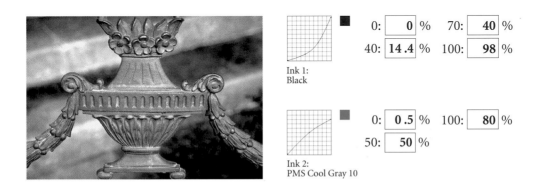

Ink 1:
Black

0: [0] %   70: [40] %
40: [14.4] % 100: [98] %

Ink 2:
PMS Cool Gray 10

0: [0.5] %   100: [80] %
50: [50] %

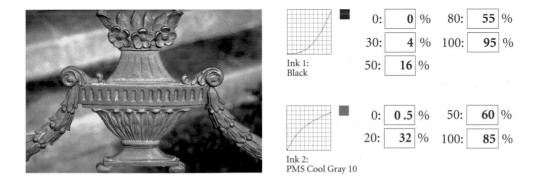

Ink 1:
Black

0: [0] %   80: [55] %
30: [4] %   100: [95] %
50: [16] %

Ink 2:
PMS Cool Gray 10

0: [0.5] %   50: [60] %
20: [32] %   100: [85] %

Duotones (*continued*)

Printing Inks:

Ink 1:
Black

Ink 2:
PMS 485

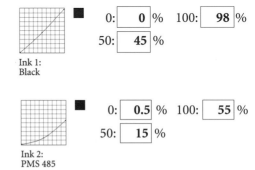

Ink 1:
Black

0: **0** %   100: **98** %

50: **45** %

0: **0.5** %   100: **55** %

50: **15** %

Ink 2:
PMS 485

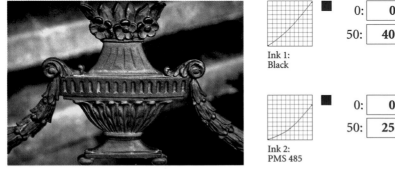

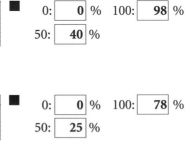

Ink 1:
Black

0: **0** %   100: **98** %

50: **40** %

0: **0** %   100: **78** %

50: **25** %

Ink 2:
PMS 485

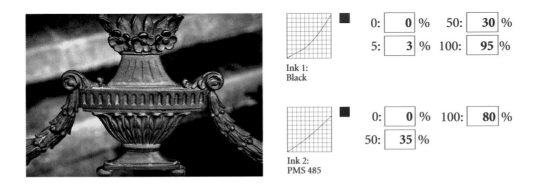

Ink 1:
Black

0: **0** %   50: **30** %
5: **3** %   100: **95** %

Ink 2:
PMS 485

0: **0** %   100: **80** %
50: **35** %

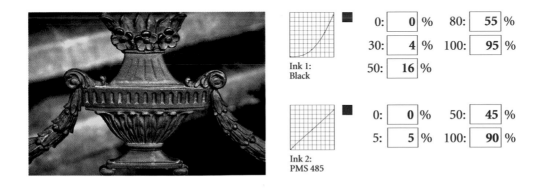

Ink 1:
Black

0: **0** %   80: **55** %
30: **4** %   100: **95** %
50: **16** %

Ink 2:
PMS 485

0: **0** %   50: **45** %
5: **5** %   100: **90** %

Tritones

Printing Inks:

Ink 1:
Black

Ink 2:
PMS Cool
Gray 10

Ink 3:
PMS Cool Gray 1

Ink 1:
Black

0:	**0** %	80:	**40** %
50:	**5** %	100:	**100** %

Ink 2:
PMS Cool Gray 10

0:	**0** %	50:	**30.5** %
20:	**12** %	100:	**95** %

Ink 3:
PMS Cool Gray 1

0:	**0** %	100:	**100** %
40:	**73.8** %		

Ink 1:
Black

0:	**0** %	50:	**10** %
30:	**2** %	100:	**70** %

Ink 2:
PMS Cool Gray 10

0:	**5** %	100:	**80** %
50:	**20** %		

Ink 3:
PMS Cool Gray 1

0:	**10** %	100:	**100** %
50:	**80** %		

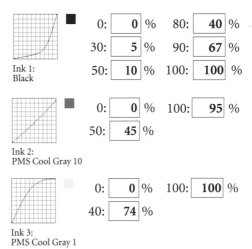

Ink 1:
Black

0: 0 %   80: 40 %

30: 5 %   90: 67 %

50: 10 %   100: 100 %

Ink 2:
PMS Cool Gray 10

0: 0 %   100: 95 %

50: 45 %

Ink 3:
PMS Cool Gray 1

0: 0 %   100: 100 %

40: 74 %

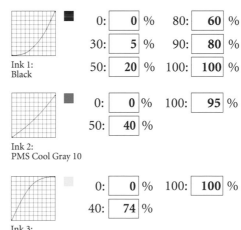

Ink 1:
Black

0: 0 %   80: 60 %

30: 5 %   90: 80 %

50: 20 %   100: 100 %

Ink 2:
PMS Cool Gray 10

0: 0 %   100: 95 %

50: 40 %

Ink 3:
PMS Cool Gray 1

0: 0 %   100: 100 %

40: 74 %

Simplifying Vector Graphics

The complexity of an illustration can dramatically affect how it images on an output device. Creating line art efficiently in Adobe Illustrator or other vector-based software programs reduces imaging time and imaging errors. Efficient illustration techniques reduce the amount of memory and time needed to image a publication. These techniques can also contribute to smaller files, faster screen redraw, and easier editing.

Prepress service providers may charge extra to image a file that takes longer than a standard time to output, or they may delay imaging your file so that it doesn't hold up other jobs. The more you can reduce the amount of processing time required for your file, the more you control the schedule and cost of your job.

In general, curves require more imaging time and memory than do straight lines. This is because when output on raster devices, curves are actually represented by multiple tiny straight-line segments. Likewise, paths in illustrations print faster when you use the fewest points possible.

The *flatness* of the curve determines the length of individual segments. A curve with little flatness is constructed of a large number of very short segments. Increasing the flatness will cause the curve to be approximated by fewer and longer segments, and may make the individual segments noticeable; however, it will also make illustrations print faster.

If text is used in an illustration, the illustration program can extract and store the outlines of individual letters as paths. These letter outlines can speed printing by making it unnecessary for the output device to download the font. When an illustration contains type that has been altered or manipulated using fills, rotations, or transformations, consider converting the type to outlines. This may slightly change the character shape. Avoid converting small type to outlines because the type may become unreadable.

Tips for simplifying illustrations

- Avoid multiple graphic or text effects in a single object. Rotating and transforming a bitmap image and masking it with a complex path will cause the object to print slowly.

- Delete any object you can't see in preview mode. All objects on printing layers process when you print, even if they are hidden behind other objects.

- Optimum flatness values depend on the complexity of the paths you have created and the output resolution. See the user guide for your software program for more information on setting flatness levels for illustrations.

- Because masking is memory-intensive, simplify the path and the object you want to mask.

- Crop and rotate illustrations before importing them into your page-layout program.

- Use text on a path sparingly.

- Limit the number of typefaces in your publication.

- Limit the number of gradients and patterns in your illustrations.

- Avoid rotating, scaling, or skewing patterns; create them at the size and angle that they will print.

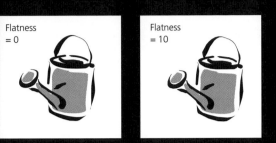

Flatness
= 0

Flatness
= 10

Higher flatness values cause objects to print faster.

Simplified paths print faster.

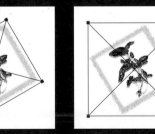

Bitmap images print faster when rotated in an image-editing application before they are imported.

Image Editing and Interpolation

Rasterizing an image essentially involves mapping the image onto a raster grid by filling in the color of each pixel. Think of laying a blank grid over the image, as if you were going to trace it, and choosing a color for each pixel. If you are working with a particular color model, such as RGB, filling in the color of a pixel means choosing color levels.

During editing, an image that has already been mapped out on one grid may need to be remapped by the computer onto a different-sized grid, or rotated and mapped back onto a grid the same size. Editing often involves selecting some portion of the image, making a geometrical change in it such as rotation or enlargement, and projecting it back on the raster. In an image-editing program, remapping is a basic routine on which many other operations depend.

Usually, when a raster image needs to be projected onto a new grid, some form of *interpolation*—a scheme for generating intermediate values—is performed to determine the color levels for each pixel in the new grid. Imagine superimposing a fresh blank raster on a rotated image as if you were going to trace the rotated image, and imagine how you might proceed to fill in color at each pixel in the new grid. Since a new pixel will not usually coincide with one in the old grid, but is more likely to overlap, or be neighbors with, several

in the old grid, you would probably need a way of averaging nearby colors in the underlying old one. You might invent other ways to reach a compromise among neighboring levels, besides straightforward averaging. Any reasonable way of calculating color levels for a pixel in the new grid that takes account of nearby values in the underlying old grid could be viewed as a method of interpolation.

Adobe Photoshop, for example, lets you select from three methods of interpolation: Nearest Neighbor, Bilinear, and Bicubic. Nearest Neighbor is the fastest and simplest method but yields the least subtle results. Bicubic is the most sophisticated and memory-intensive interpolation method and should be used when exacting quality is required.

Continous-tone image

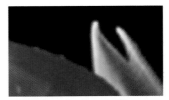

Enlarged section using Bicubic

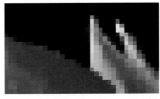

Enlarged section using Nearest Neighbor

Grayscale image

Enlarged section using Bicubic

Enlarged section using Nearest Neighbor

Pixelated image

Enlarged section using Bicubic

Enlarged section using Nearest Neighbor

Scaling and Resampling

A raster image contains a fixed number of pixels, and the dimensions at which it will be displayed or printed determine its resolution, or pixels per inch.

Resampling occurs when you change the number of pixels in the raster used to display an image. This alters the file's information content without implying any decision to change the dimensions for display or printing. Resampling up or down is accomplished in effect by projecting an image on a fresh grid with a different number of pixels.

It is tempting to describe upsampling as jamming fresh pixels into an existing grid and choosing neighbors for them to emulate, but it doesn't happen that way. Nor is downsampling done by knocking some pixels out of an existing grid and closing ranks to eliminate gaps. When an image is projected onto a fresh grid with a different number of pixels, or scaled or skewed and projected onto a new area of the old grid, interpolation is used to construct color levels for the pixels in the new grid.

Downsampling is sometimes done intentionally to reduce the bulk of an image file, making it less time-consuming for the system to handle. But resampling, either up or down, can also happen unintentionally as a result of scaling some or all of an image.

In an image-editing program such as Photoshop you can use various tools to select a part of the image on the screen. Once an object has been selected, and its selection boundaries have appeared on the screen, you can manipulate it in various ways: rotate, enlarge, shrink, stretch, or compress along a chosen axis, and so on. The manipulated object is automatically mapped back into the overall grid. Since the pixel size does not change in this case, shrinking an object has the effect of automatically downsampling it. A smaller size on the screen corresponds to fewer pixels.

Here are some things to remember about scaling and resampling raster images:

- In general it is best to scan an image at the scale and resolution you need it, to avoid having either to resample or to resize.

200-ppi scan resolution; 869K file size

100-ppi scan resolution; 386K file size

Scaling and Resampling *(continued)*

- You can increase the resolution of a raster image by fitting it into a smaller space. Doing that does not involve any change in the size of the image's file, and does not involve resampling.

- Downsampling for printing works best if you divide the original resolution by a whole number. For instance, if your original image was 600 ppi, resample to make the new resolution a simple fraction of 600 ppi such as 300, 150, or 75 ppi.

- Once an image is downsampled, the original information cannot be recovered except by rescanning. Resampling down and then up deteriorates the quality of an image.

- Upsampling is rarely a good idea. The result is apt to be fuzzy or soft-edged. For the same reason, an image that looks good small may not be satisfactory when enlarged, even when upsampling has been performed.

- Using a sharpening filter, such as the Unsharp Mask filter in Photoshop, compensates for some of the blurring introduced by scanning, resampling, and printing.

A   B   C

A. Resampled down   B. Original   C. Resampled up

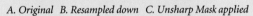

A   B   C

A. Original   B. Resampled down   C. Unsharp Mask applied

Graphic File Formats

The file format you choose for your graphics depends on your workflow and final output.

The EPS (Encapsulated PostScript) file format can contain vector graphics or raster images. EPS is used to transport PostScript information between programs on the Macintosh and Windows platforms. These files contain a screen preview, instructions for a PostScript output device, and in some cases raster image data. Adobe Illustrator saves artwork in EPS format; Adobe PageMaker can create EPS files of a single publication's pages.

The TIFF™ file format is used for storing black-and-white, grayscale, or color raster images. There are three common types of TIFF images: RGB TIFF images store colors in the RGB color model; CMYK TIFF images contain preseparated image data designed for printing color separations; and Lab TIFFs contain raster image data stored in a device-independent color model called CIE L*a*b. The TIFF format is used for exchanging raster images between applications on the Macintosh and Windows platforms.

Photo CD files contain raster images in several resolutions and are stored on a special CD in YCC format. Photo CD files can store images from 35mm, 70mm, 120mm, and 4-by-5-inch film formats. Photo CD is an efficient format for digitally storing photographs and slides.

Desktop Color Separation (DCS) files are EPS files that combine a low-resolution display image with high-resolution data for color separations. DCS 1.0 files are composed of five parts—a low-resolution file for placement, and separations files for cyan, magenta, yellow, and black. DCS 2.0 supports additional options and convenience: Spot color separations can be included; all the separations can be stored in a single file; and two low-resolution files are included, an RGB version for placement and a CMYK version for low-resolution color proofing.

DCS file —

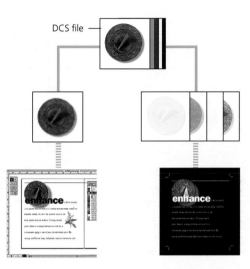

Low-resolution file used for placement

Separation files used for output

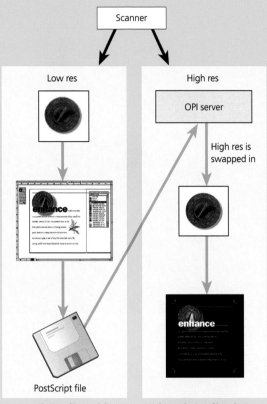

Scanner

Low res

High res

OPI server

High res is
swapped in

*Low-resolution file used for
placement*

PostScript file

*High-resolution file substituted
for separations*

Open Prepress Interface

Open Prepress Interface (OPI™) is an extension of PostScript that is particularly suited to working with large files containing high-resolution images. In this kind of project you may not have desktop storage capable of holding all the images and may have to leave files at the point where you have them scanned and where they will be imaged.

When you use an application that supports OPI, your service provider can scan your artwork, keep the high-resolution image, and give you a low-resolution placeholder version to use in design and layout. You do not need the large storage capacity or fast processing speed required to store and edit high-resolution TIFF images, which range in size from several megabytes to 50 megabytes.

When you have created your publication using a page-layout program that supports OPI, you or your service provider can generate a PostScript file containing OPI comments, which specify the page, placement, size, and cropping of any TIFF images. Your prepress service provider uses a prepress application that automatically substitutes the high-resolution versions of the TIFF images before imaging.

Managing Linked Graphics

Linking builds a reference to an image or illustration file without including the file in a publication. This space-saving technique is useful when you work with large graphic files like raster images or EPS graphics. When you link to a graphic, the application places a low-resolution version of the graphic in your document as a placeholder for display and keeps track of where the high-resolution version is stored. When you print the document, the application locates the original graphic file on disk and uses it instead of the low-resolution version. Linking reduces your document file size, but if the original file cannot be located, the low-resolution placeholder prints, probably yielding disappointing results.

Adobe PageMaker and Adobe Illustrator identify linked files using their filenames and locations; therefore it's important to keep track of your linked files. Organize your files as you construct your document by setting up folders for your linked or placed art. Well-organized files make the eventual handoff to the prepress service provider easier and can save time and money. Always verify that links are up to date before imaging a file.

As an alternative to linking, raster images and illustrations can be stored within a document. When you store a graphic in a document, a complete copy of the graphic file is included in the document, thereby increasing the size of the file. The advantage of storing graphics within a publication is that the high-resolution version of the graphic is always available when the file is imaged.

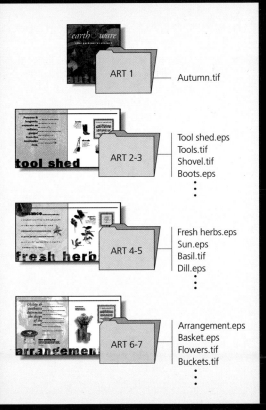

Organize your files as you construct your publication by setting up folders for art.

Using Type

In the world of electronic production, type should look good on-screen and print flawlessly from output devices such as laser printers and imagesetters. Unlike type that is cast in metal or imaged photographically, digital type gives you the means to control every aspect of typesetting.

When you buy an Adobe typeface for either the Macintosh or Windows platform, Adobe Type Manager (ATM) is also included. A basic understanding of how type renders on-screen and in print using ATM will help you produce more eloquent printed pages.

Typesetting terms

When older typesetting methods gave way to desktop publishing, certain traditional terms got tangled in the process. This discussion is intended to clarify the meanings of some common type terms that have been misused or have broader meanings than they did in the days of metal or photoset type.

Typefaces. The basic building block in typesetting is a character—a letter, number, or symbol; groups of characters are called character sets. One or more character sets sharing particular design features make up a typeface design; Adobe Caslon, for example, is the name of a typeface design.

A complete character set reflecting one stylistic variation of a typeface design, such as italic or bold, is known as a typestyle (see also "Fonts" below). Basic typestyles may be combined to form new ones, such as the Adobe Caslon Bold Italic typestyle shown here. (This is the standard character set for the Macintosh; the character set you can access depends on your application and your hardware platform.)

ABCDEFGHIJKLMNOPQRSTUVWXYZ

abcdefghijklmnopqrstuvwxyz&0123456789

ÆÅÁÂÄÀÃÇÉÊËÈÍÎÏÌÑŒÓÔÖÒÕØÚ

ÛÜÙæáâäàãçéêëèWXíîïìñœóôöò߀úûüù

ÿ£¥$¢¤™©®@ᵃᵒ†‡§¶!¡?¿.,:;ᵒᵏᵒᵖ...’”◊«»()[]*

ß\/——-•´‘‘◊~~´^,,#%‰=-+~<±>÷¬°^/·

Adobe Caslon Bold Italic typestyle

When several typestyles share a particular typeface design, they make up a typeface family. The Adobe Caslon typeface family, for instance, is made up of regular, italic, bold, and other typestyles of the Adobe Caslon typeface design.

A multiple master typeface is essentially one typeface family from which hundreds of stylistic variations, called multiple master instances, can be generated.

Fonts. In traditional metal type, font described a single point size of a particular typestyle and typeface design. Because digital-typesetting technology enables scalable fonts, however, today the size distinction is not always applicable. For example, Adobe Caslon Italic as a whole is considered both a scalable font and a typestyle; each instance of a multiple master typeface is also a scalable font and a typestyle.

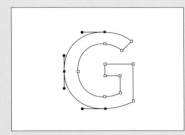

Outline (printer) font

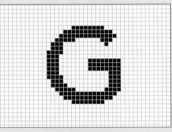

Bitmap (screen) font

Outline fonts, also known as printer fonts, are the means by which digital type is scalable. (On the Windows platform, outline fonts are called .pfb files [primary font binary].) They are created using code that describes the ideal outline of each character in mathematical terms. By adjusting the mathematical formulas, your computer can scale the point size of a character without distortion. Outline fonts generate smooth output. As with all digital images, fonts are displayed on-screen as bitmap representations; thus, bitmap fonts are sometimes referred to as screen fonts. Each letter is built using a pattern of dots (pixels) that together represent the letter at a specific point size. On the Macintosh, bitmap fonts are often kept in font "suitcases." On a Windows platform, bitmap fonts are created dynamically by ATM.

Adobe Type Manager

The Adobe Type Manager font utility automatically generates any size bitmap font from outline-font data. By rasterizing the outlines, ATM translates them into digital bitmaps so they can be represented on-screen. With ATM, you can scale, rotate, and skew type without the characters appearing jagged (the degree of smoothness is determined by the monitor resolution). ATM also lets you print Type 1 fonts on non-PostScript printers.

Printer memory

A PostScript printer's random access memory (RAM) is used to store downloaded fonts, to scale fonts, and to render an entire page of a document.

Macintosh 72-dpi screen display without ATM

Macintosh 72-dpi screen display with ATM

Virtual memory. Only a portion of a printer's total memory, known as virtual memory, is available for storage of downloadable fonts. The amount of virtual memory varies from printer to printer, but in most cases you can increase it by adding more RAM. Contact your printer manufacturer first, though, because there may be a maximum amount of virtual memory that can be created, regardless of total RAM. You can also store fonts on a hard drive attached to your printer, which will free up the printer's virtual memory.

Also keep in mind that multiple master fonts are apt to use considerably more virtual memory than their corresponding non-multiple master fonts. For example, the ITC Avant Garde Book typestyle requires 28K of virtual memory, while the ITC Avant Garde Gothic multiple master font needs 68K (each additional instance requires only about 3K more virtual memory). See page 127 for information on multiple master fonts.

Searching for Fonts

When you send a document to a PostScript printer, the printer uses the fonts it finds according to the following priorities:

1. Fonts that have been manually downloaded to the printer's RAM.

2. Fonts stored in the read-only memory (ROM) of the printer.

3. Fonts stored on a hard disk in or attached to the printer.

4. Fonts stored in the Macintosh or Windows system (these are downloaded by the printer driver when the job is sent to the printer).

5. Courier if the printer cannot find the font in any of these other locations.

If you're going to use

ugly typefaces

at all, then use them

with mucho gusto!

Be brave!

Make a statement!

Yes, this is

an ugly typeface!

–Robin Williams,
Santa Fe, NM

Setting Good-Looking Type

A sculpture's success depends not only on its shape and material, but also on the space around it. Typography is no different—to communicate ideas, type must be readable as well as legible. Legibility refers to the ability to distinguish between letters; readability to ease of comprehension and reader comfort. Making type more readable involves the manipulation of space around letters, words, and lines of text.

Spacing letters

As we read a line of text, our eyes scan the upper third of the letters. From this information, we identify the overall word shapes, which we quickly comprehend as thoughts and meaning within context. When the spaces between pairs of letters (letterfit) are optically even overall, letterforms are more easily identifiable, making text more readable.

The characteristics that make a letter legible are shape, proportion, stroke contrast, and letterfit. Although the unique shape of an individual letter helps make it legible, it may also create undesirable letterfit. Thus, the spatial relationship between two or more characters is a major factor in determining a word's readability.

Multiple Master Fonts

Although it's best to avoid a huge variety of fonts on a page, you may at times want to slightly vary a font attribute for special effects or copyfitting needs. Multiple master font technology enables you to generate precisely the typeface variation you need.

Each multiple master font consists of two parts: the multiple master font itself (called the base font) and one or more *instances* of the font. An instance is a particular rendition of the font along a particular design axis, such as weight, width, style, or optical size. A multiple master font may include up to four design axes that you can use to create an almost infinite variety of font instances.

Each multiple master font also includes a collection of ready-to-use primary instances that constitute a complete typeface family. The typeface designer or manufacturer determines the selection of primary instances to provide a useful palette of fonts.

	CONDENSED					EXTENDED
LIGHT	W	W	W	W	W	W
	W	W	W	W	W	W
	W	W	W	W	W	W
	W	W	W	W	W	W
	W	W	W	W	W	W
BLACK	W	W	W	W	W	W

	CONDENSED	NORMAL	SEMI-EXTENDED
LIGHT	abc	abc	abc
REGULAR	abc	abc	abc
SEMIBOLD	abc	abc	abc
BOLD	abc	abc	abc
BLACK	abc	abc	abc

Optical size and spacing
For most digital typefaces, overall letterspacing is optimized for 12-point text. Smaller sizes (especially 8 points or less) often require added letterspacing; larger sizes need less. The optical size design axis in a multiple master typeface will make these as well as default word-space adjustments automatically.

Letterfit. To help you determine the proper spacing between any two letters, envision the space within a letterform (its counterform) and the space between it and its neighbor (its letterfit) as physical volumes. The default letterfit of most text typefaces tries to visually balance these volumes so that an even rhythm of white space is achieved.

The shapes of individual letters influence letterfit. For instance, two letters with either curved or diagonal strokes that are set together require the least amount of space between them; combinations of straight vertical lines need the most space; and a curved or diagonal stroke next to a straight line needs a medium amount of space.

The amount of space between letters depends on the shapes of the letter strokes.

Tracking. Adding or removing an equal amount of space between characters, usually in blocks of text, to achieve overall tighter or looser letterspacing is known as tracking. Type smaller than 10 points might require added space (positive tracking), while larger type sizes—say, over 18 points—might need less (negative tracking). Most page-layout programs include tracking capabilities; the way you perform this function varies by application, so refer to your user guide for details.

A Crow, half-dead with thirst, came upon a Pitcher which had once been full of water, but when the Crow put its beak into the mouth of the Pitcher

Tracking: –25 (Octavian MT, 18 points)

A Crow, half-dead with thirst, came upon a Pitcher which had once been full of water, but when the Crow put its beak into the mouth of the Pitcher he found that only very little water was left and that he could not reach far enough down to get at it. He tried, and tried, but at last had to give up in despair. Then a thought came to him, and he

Tracking: +12 (Octavian MT, 10 points)

igjen

ok

ABCDEFGHIJKLMNOPQRSTUVWXY
abcdefghijklmnopqrstuvwxyz&01234567
ÆÅÀÂÄÀÃÇÉÊËÈÍÎÏÌÑŒÓÓÔÕÖØÚ
ÛÜÙ æáâäàåãçéêëè WXíîïìñœóôöòßúûüù
…‰¢£¥ƒ¤™©®@ªº†‡§¶*!¡?¿.,.:;''«»‹› … '''◊‹«»()[]
^ˆˇ`~¯˘˙¨°˝˛˜ #%‰=-+~<±>÷¬°

ABCDEFGHIJKLMNOPQRSTUVWXYZ
abcdefghijklmnopqrstuvwxyz&0123456789
ÆÅÀÂÄÀÃÇÉÊËÈÍÎÏÌÑŒÓÓÔÕÖØÚ
ÛÜÙ æáâäàåãçéêëè WXíîïìñœóôöòßúûüù
ýŁ¥$¢¤™©®@ªº†‡§¶*!¡?¿.,.''''' … '''◊‹«»()[]
{}|\—– •.,'"‹›''""""
·/√∪└÷<±>~+=∞%‰#;

Tracking: –40 (Inflex Bold, 28/36)

Tracking: –20 (Inflex Bold, 28/36)

Reversed type, such as white type on a black background, might also require more space between letters. In this case, use positive tracking (or less negative tracking, as shown here) to improve legibility.

Your printing environment may also require adjustment of the overall letterspacing. If you are printing on an absorbent paper, for instance, you may need to increase letterspacing to allow for ink spread that occurs during printing. If so, use positive tracking.

Kerning. Altering the space between any two characters is known as kerning. Many problematic character combinations are adjusted by the typeface designer or manufacturer; these kerning pairs are included with the typeface software. Most Adobe typefaces, for instance, have 294 standard kerning pairs; Adobe Originals designs have many more—sometimes thousands.

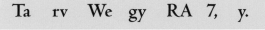

Unkerned character pairs (Centaur MT, 20 points)

Kerned character pairs (Centaur MT, 20 points)

Many applications let you kern letter pairs manually; some are also capable of using the built-in kerning pairs automatically. If your application allows it and does not do so already, make sure the built-in kerning pairs are accessible as the default in the application.

Manual kerning. At times you may need to kern manually to balance the letterfit with the counterforms for visual consistency. You may need to kern, for example, if you use all capitals or if you work with unusual letter combinations.

Capital letters are generally designed to fit well with lowercase letters, and so may look tight or uneven when set together. Nevertheless, there are times when all capitals best convey your message, though they will undoubtedly require adjustment. As always, try to balance the letters' counterforms with the space around them, first by globally tracking the words or lines of text, then by kerning the spaces between certain pairs of characters.

The following pair of examples shows manually kerned spacing between capital letters. In the first example, the capital letters are set using default spacing; in the second (after kerning and tracking), the spaces between the letter pairs are more evenly balanced with the counterforms.

CLIMATE

Before manual kerning: uneven letterfit (Adobe Caslon Regular)

CLIMATE

After manual kerning and tracking: more balanced spacing (Adobe Caslon Regular)

Unusual letter combinations, which crop up in work with languages other than English or in situations in which there are no predefined kerning pairs, can cause letters to tangle, distracting the eye. Add space where letters "crash," as shown in this example (*igjen* is the Norwegian word for again).

igjen

Before kerning (Adobe Caslon Semibold)

igjen

After kerning (Adobe Caslon Semibold)

Spacing words

Words need to be far enough apart to be distinguished from one another, but not so far that they separate into individual, unrelated units. The spaces between words have to be large enough to see individual word shapes, but the reader must also be able to group three or four words at a time for quick comprehension. The proper word spacing for unjustified text (in which the right margin is uneven or ragged) depends primarily on type size and line length.

If headlines are set in a large-size type—24 points, for example—little space is required between words; the space used by a 24-point lowercase i is a good gauge. In typical 12-point body text of ten words per line, however, more space between words is required. Most page-layout programs use the default word spacing provided in each typeface, which usually works well without adjustment in typical text settings, and some allow you to adjust this spacing. Very short lines of text require tighter word spacing than the default.

A Jay ventured into a yard

Headline word spacing (Myriad multiple master 700 weight 500 width, 24 points)

If one spacing parameter changes on the page, then the others should change accordingly. If you increase the spaces between the words and letters, for instance, you need to increase the leading as well.

Create close relationships with knowlegdeable and experienced production people, print brokers, and service bureaus. You can benefit from the combined expertise.

–Lori Barra,
TonBo designs, Sausalito, CA

Choosing a Font Format

Choosing the type of font to work with is the first step in making sure the type on your pages displays and prints correctly. The two main font standards are PostScript Type 1 and TrueType.

Competing font standards make selecting fonts an important decision: The same typeface design may be available in a PostScript font and a TrueType font. The visual characteristics of one font standard differ slightly from another. Because of this difference, using one type of font for displaying and proofing your work and then using a different font for printing can cause unpleasant surprises like different letterspacing and line endings.

PostScript fonts are the industry standard for imaging to any PostScript output device. PostScript fonts are PostScript language-based outlines—object-oriented vector graphics—that can be scaled to any size, and still remain sharp and smooth on any platform, or output device.

TrueType fonts work well with non-PostScript and PostScript output devices. The disadvantage of using TrueType fonts when printing to a PostScript printer is that the font must be converted to a PostScript outline; the quality of the resulting font depends on the quality of the conversion.

When creating a publication with double-byte characters, such as those found in Asian or Arabic character sets, talk with your prepress service provider to determine if the imagesetter can support the double-byte font required.

For most efficient printing, choose a font that does not have to be converted on your final output device, and use only one font standard in your publication.

Whatever font standard you choose, talk with your prepress service provider about the fonts you intend to use. Specify the name of the font, the company that made the font, and whether the fonts are in PostScript or TrueType format. Make sure you and your service provider use the same fonts.

Fonts from different manufacturers may not have the same characteristics even if they share the same font name.

"CONNIE IN THE F

WILLIAM F

OIL ON CANV
UNSIGNED, HAS F

THE ART OF THE GARDEN WAS PRINTED using a traditional four-color process and two spot colors. According to Mirelez, "the two spot colors were chosen strictly on aesthetics. The only consideration was that they be dark enough to hold up as text type. Other than that, they merely had to look good with all the other graphics." The two spot colors were chosen near the end of the design process.

To save money, Mirelez did not use a varnish, but chose a dull, coated paper stock that contrasted with the ink's gloss, thereby achieving the same effect as a varnish.

Because he had reviewed the publication with his printer, and the printer had provided him with an actual-size dummy of the publication, Mirelez was able to design the publication efficiently. The interior of the catalog was designed to print on two 16-page signatures, and was then hand-collated and stapled. The binding cover was glued on by hand.

Don't trust your monitor

for correcting scans. Take an extra five

minutes to compare your

screen color values with the same values in

a CMYK swatch book.

–Andrew Faulkner,
Andrew Faulkner Design, San Francisco, CA

3

Imaging and Proofing

Desktop proofing options

When to convert to PostScript

Checking your files

Including a written report

Inspecting film from the imagesetter

Color proofing

Checking press proofs

Color bars

Printing via Web

Single-format workflow

Archiving in PDF

Real-world project

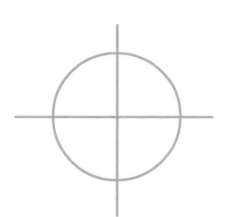

Imaging and Proofing

Checking your finished files, handing them off for transfer to film, and proofing the results are three key steps in the final production cycle.

A final check prior to handoff will ordinarily include printing a trial copy on your desktop printer. Inspecting a desktop copy is hardly the same as getting actual proofs from the press, but it can be thought of as the first of several stages of proofing. Prior to handoff it is equally important to verify that your files are complete on the portable disk drive or disk cartridge serving as the vehicle between you and the imagesetter.

Turning over your files for imaging involves organizing them on portable storage and preparing written notes to go with them. Handoff is a step where communication with your service provider is critical. The location and labeling of all files, including linked art and fonts, must be clear to your service provider for the handoff to be successful. Preparing your files so that another person can take charge of them, and assembling the written report to go with them, serve to identify any points needing clarification.

A production run will usually be contingent on your being satisfied with all or some of the following: sheets of film produced by imaging the files, film-based color proofs, and press proofs.

Desktop Proofing Options

Preview your publication throughout its development as a way to check the layout, verify the accuracy of text and graphics, and solve potential printing problems before the files are imaged. If you are creating a four-color process publication, you can preview each of the separations using a black-and-white printer to see if objects print on the correct separations. A color desktop printer can be used to print a composite giving a rough idea of the combined effect of all four colors.

Problems identified in an early preview or desktop proof can be corrected easily; the same problems identified on film separations are more time-consuming and expensive to fix. Also, many prepress service providers require PostScript laser printer separations when you deliver electronic files for imaging.

Intersperse preview and proofing cycles into your workflow as you develop your publication. When you find a mistake in your publication, correct the problem and verify the changes by proofing on the desktop before imaging film. If you plan to produce separations, print two sets of laser copies: one separated and one composite.

TYPE OF PROOF

On-screen (soft proof)

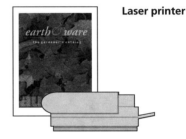

Laser printer

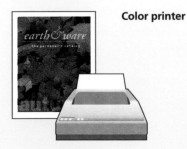

Color printer

WHAT IT IS

An on-screen preview lets you examine the pages of your publication displayed on a monitor.

Black-and-white copies of each of your four color separations and of the composite image are printed on a PostScript laser printer. This is an inexpensive way to identify problems with layout and design, and to verify that objects have been assigned to the correct color separations.

With certain caveats, a color composite printed on a PostScript color printer can be regarded as a type of proof. High-resolution (720-1440 dpi), low-cost inkjet printers can also generate good preliminary proofs.

Direct digital color proofs are gaining acceptance, and for some jobs may be used as contract proofs—proofs that indicate to the commercial printer the color that you expect in the final document.

APPROPRIATE USES

Use to refine the appearance of text and to check the overall layout. Enlarge critical areas to get a better look. Check to see that the intended colors have been assigned to each object. Don't rely on the on-screen appearance of colors unless you are using a color management system (CMS).

Use a composite proof to preview your layout and text. Create separated proofs to see whether objects occur on the appropriate separations and whether they knock out or overprint as specified. Check for registration marks and crop marks.

Printing on a laser printer can alert you to problems you may encounter on an imagesetter, assuming that both are PostScript devices. Files generating PostScript errors on one will probably generate errors on the other. Non-PostScript printers are less suitable for this purpose.

Composites from a desktop color printer can be useful for previewing overall page design, showing color relationships, and verifying bitmap image resolution. These composites have the disadvantage of not letting you anticipate some common press problems, such as moiré patterns. Also, most color composites cannot accurately show traps.

Unless you have been using a CMS with accurately calibrated ICC profiles, the colors may be unreliable.

When to Convert to PostScript

Assuming that you have created your document in a page-layout program, your files are in the format that is specific to that particular application. At handoff you may choose to transfer your files as they are—in PageMaker format if you have been working in PageMaker—and let the service bureau make the conversion to PostScript, or you may choose to convert your files yourself. There are advantages to either approach.

Transferring files in their native form

Handing off a file in the format of your page-layout program allows the service bureau to run its own preflight check on your file, making sure that linked files are found and that necessary fonts are available. Your service provider can also select the correct printing options for the job: emulsion settings, printer's marks, screen ruling, and any additional settings. If service providers encounter problems, they can troubleshoot the files and fix them. Keep in mind that vendors generally charge for the time they spend fixing file problems.

If your service provider will be doing the trapping for you, format may make a difference. Trapping can be done in PostScript files, but many service providers prefer to perform the task in a page-layout program and create the PostScript file when they are finished.

Before you hand off in a page-layout program, make sure that you and your prepress service provider use the same version. An older version may not open files made in a more recent one, or may not support key features. Different versions may treat some file characteristics differently, producing unexpected results. If you are using different versions, or for that matter different computer platforms, consult with your service provider on how to proceed.

Doing the conversion to PostScript yourself

In the event that your service provider doesn't use the same page-layout program you do, or uses a substantially different version, you might choose to perform the conversion to PostScript yourself. If your service provider doesn't have certain fonts you want in your publication, one solution is to generate a PostScript file including the required fonts. You may also choose to convert your files to PostScript simply to ensure that the job is done to your satisfaction and to reduce your dependence on the service provider.

In the conversion to PostScript, your page layout, illustrations, and bitmap images are translated into PostScript language instructions tailored to a particular output device. When you are the one making this translation, you are responsible for entering the correct settings for the job. Your service provider or commercial printer can tell you the proper settings based on what they know about the imaging device.

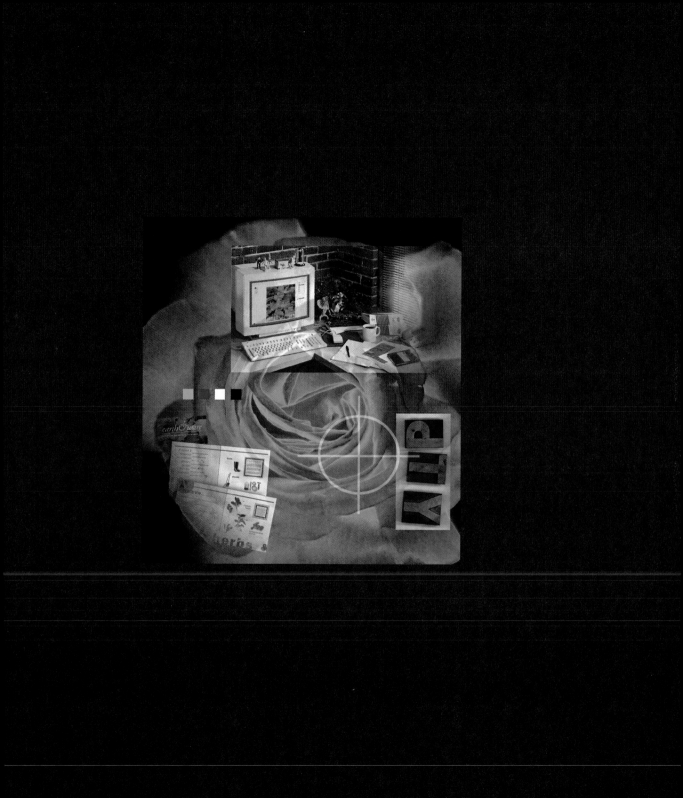

Checking Your Files

When it's time to hand off your document to your prepress service provider, a systematic check of your files helps ensure that your document will print from another computer. This process, analogous to a pilot's preflight check, is intended to catch missing files, missing fonts, material not intended for printing, and any components that may prevent the document from imaging properly.

After you have checked your files, organize them so that your service provider can easily find all the files required to print the publication. Make a final black-and-white proof of your files on a PostScript laser printer. If you plan to produce separations, print two sets of laser copies: one separated and one composite. Take the time to anticipate problems before you hand off files. This reduces the chance that your service provider will have to troubleshoot problems in the file and charge you for additional time required to prepare the file for imaging.

Checking files before imaging

- For multiple-page publications, delete unnecessary pages.

- Check linked graphics to ensure that you are using the latest versions.

- Make sure that your print and document settings are appropriate for the final output device. Often print settings must be changed to proof the publication on a laser printer, so check that all settings are correct for your service provider's imagesetter.

- Use the right PPD for final output. A PPD file contains information for a particular PostScript output device that ensures the best possible results when imaging color separations.

- Verify that your colors are defined and named correctly. If you are using spot colors, make sure that each is defined with just one name.

- Check bleeds and traps. Make sure that bleed allowances are sufficient, and that trap specifications are correct.

Organizing files on the portable medium

- Copy all art, publication, and bitmap image files required onto the medium you will use to hand off the files to your prepress service provider. Storage media such as portable hard disks or removable cartridges are excellent for transferring large amounts of data.

- Use a data-compression program to temporarily reduce the size of your files if you are working with large image files. Be sure to check your program's documentation to find out what type of compression is best for your needs.

- Gather your final laser proofs, your prepress service provider report, and the assembled files. This is the packet you will hand to your service provider.

145

Including a Report

Plan to give a written report of all the requirements and settings for your document to your prepress service provider. The report not only helps you visualize your document from your vendor's point of view, but it gives your service provider and commercial printer an understanding of your expectations. Some shops have a form for you to fill out and submit with your files. The report you have prepared can be submitted attached to their form.

Your service provider report should be an orderly listing of the details of your document. For small projects, notes written on a printout of the thumbnails of your document should be sufficient. For multiple-page publications, the report should account for every page in your publication, including blank pages, that will be bound in the printed piece. Include a printed hard copy and pagination sheet with all projects. If the piece folds, include a folded laser output version, called a folding dummy.

In addition to your service provider report, you should include a specification sheet for your commercial printer. The specification sheet should include the publication specifications information shown here, as well as the following information:

- Carton weight and packaging specifications

- Due date and delivery instructions

- Deliverable specifications (number of boards, disks, samples, etc.)

- Film storage and ownership information

- Quoted price from printer

Sample service provider report

Settings for imaging
List print settings you've agreed to with your prepress service provider, such as output resolution, ICC profiles used, PPD used, screen ruling, dot gain settings, UCR or GCR settings, and trap tolerance. Indicate film settings including emulsion orientation and whether the film is set to be positive or negative. If applicable, list the color management system and device profiles used.

Font list
List all fonts used in the document and any fonts that were included in imported artwork.

Detailed page listing
List all pages in your publication, including both blank and numbered pages. Use the page numbers to keep track of special requirements on each page. Indicate sections, chapters, or other breaks in long publications.

Filenames and location of artwork
Give the name of each document or PostScript file. For multiple file documents, list component files. List DCS files and mention any extra spot separations. Indicate the location of low- and high-resolution images and any artwork in the originating application format.

Separations
If you are printing color, indicate the number of separations that need to be made for each page. This number should also include any spot colors or varnishes on the page.

Notes
Include short memos to remind you of any special situations on the page. List the location of all bleeds, crossovers, manually stripped-in images, and areas in the publication that need special attention. Indicate if the graphics on the page have been trapped.

Earth & Ware Catalog
Contact name: _____

Date: _____
Phone: _____

Publication specifications

Cover:

- 10 x 15 flat, 10 x 7.5 folded
- Paper: Starbright Tierra Vellum 80 lb.
- 5-color: 4-color process, spot varnish
- Saddle stitch

Inside signature:

- 16-page signature, 7.5 x 10 trimmed
- Paper: Starbright Tierra Vellum 70 lb.
- 6-color: 4-color process,
    PANTONE 5747 and spot varnish

⟵ Commercial printer specification sheet

- PPD: Agfa Select 7000
- UCR setting: 17%

Resolution: 2400 dpi
GCR setting: none

Screen: 150 lpi
Orientation: Tall

⟵ Settings for imaging

- Fonts: Franklin Gothic-Heavy, Demi; Copperplate-32BC, 33BC; Adobe Garamond-Expert, Italic

⟵ Font list

Filename	Pages	Separations	Total	Notes
• 00 Cover.pm6 front and back	1 total	4 + varnish	5	Bleeds off all sides Inside cover is blank Art is in *Cover* folder
• 01 e&w Catalog.pm6	7 total			Art is in *ART 1* folder
page 1 (i)		4	4	
page 2 (ii)		4 + spot & varnish	6	Bleed off top of page
page 3		4 + spot & varnish	6	Bleed off top of page
page 4		4 + varnish	5	Bleed into gutter
page 5		4 + spot	5	
page 6		4 + varnish	5	Bleed into gutter
page 7		4 + spot	5	Link to high-res Herb.tif
• 02 e&w Catalog.pm6	9 total			Art is in *ART 2* folder
page 8		4 + varnish	5	Bleed into gutter
page 9		4 + spot	5	
page 10		4 + varnish	5	Basil.eps trapped in Illustrator 5.5
page 11		4 + spot	5	
page 12		4 + spot, varnish	6	
page 13		4 + spot, varnish	6	
page 14		Black + spot	2	
page 15		Black + spot	2	
page 16		4 + varnish	4	

⟵ Location of art (ART 1)

⟵ Location of art (ART 2)

Detailed page listing

Filenames

Separations

Notes

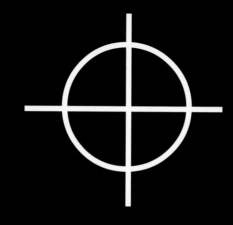

Inspecting Film from the Imagesetter

The success of your print job depends in large part on the quality of your film separations. The separation film should be checked thoroughly before you incur the expense of making color proofs.

Certain tasks necessary for checking film quality require specific equipment, such as a densitometer and a tool for measuring screen angle and ruling. Other tasks require a loupe or a keen eye for detail. Work with your prepress service provider to determine who will check the items in the following list.

What to look for on film separations

- The overall quality of the film separations. Look for streaking, scratches, or other damage to the film. Make sure that areas that should be clear aren't foggy.

- The dimensions of the publication.

- Fonts. Verify that text printed correctly.

- The screen angle and ruling for each separation.

- The objects occurring in each separation.

- Overprinting and knock-out. Check that these occurred as expected.

- Bleeds. Look to see that objects extend beyond the boundary indicated by the crop marks.

- Trapping. Verify that intended overlaps actually occur.

- The alignment of the printer's marks used for registration.

- The consistency of tints and halftones, particularly in scanned images. Check for smooth gradation carried over from the original.

- The maximum density (Dmax) of the black areas on your film separations as measured by a densitometer.

- The dot values of your tints and halftones.

If a single separation for a page is wrong, ask that all separations for that page be refilmed to ensure that the separations don't misregister.

Color Proofing

Next to proofs made on the printing plates themselves, the most accurate proofs have long been considered to be those based on the actual pieces of film that will be used to make the printing plates. These are called separation-based color proofs, or analog proofs, and are regarded as the industry standard. It is also possible to get direct digital color proofs, made with dyes or inks instead of film. Kodak, 3M, DuPont, Lino-Hell, and Scitex all manufacture high-end digital printers that proof for press.

As a general rule, the closer the proofing method mimics the conditions of the actual printing press, the more reliably it indicates the final product's quality. For color work, plan to create laminate proofs. These proofs are often used as contract proofs to indicate to the commercial printer the color that you expect in the final document. Most color proofing systems are for four-color work; a few proofing systems can also proof high-fidelity colors and spot colors. For spot colors, you can also get a *drawdown*—a smear of ink produced on the paper to be used—to verify quality and tone of a spot color. Consult your vendors to see what proofing options are available.

The final stage of proofing is not only for checking your work, but also for checking the printer's work. Without a contract proof, it may be difficult to settle disputes with the printer about color quality. A proof often serves as a guide for adjusting the press during a press check.

Correction costs continue to increase after separations are made; most changes to the publication require that the film be reproduced after corrections are made. Errors discovered during a press check are the most expensive to fix if you have to fix the problem by reproducing film and creating new printing plates. You may also have to pay for press time that was scheduled.

TYPE OF PROOF

Overlay proofs

Laminate proofs

Direct digital proofs

Bluelines

Press proofs and press checks

WHAT IT IS

Overlay proofs are created by printing film separations on acetate sheets colored to match the four process inks; the sheets are then layered on top of each other. Examples are DuPont Cromacheck and 3M Color Key.

Laminate proofs are created by representing each film separation on a layer of pigmented material, and then binding the pigmented layers together. Examples are Fuji Color-Art, DuPont Waterproof and Cromalin, 3M Matchprint, and corresponding products by Lino-Hell and Agfa.

Digital CMYK proofs are usually created using dyes or inks. High-end digital proofs are generated using lasers to burn an image onto a proofing substrate, a process similar to imagesetting.

Bluelines are photographic contact prints made from film separations. They are made on paper the same dimensions as the press sheet, and can be bound and folded so that you can check crossovers, bleeds, and page sequence. Bluelines are commonly produced for one-color or two-color publications as well as four-color process jobs.

For a press proof, preliminary film is output and the printer sets up the press to show what the actual sheet will look like. Multiple adjustments are often made and final films are generated for the print job. Press proofs are seldom done as they are costly.

A more common practice is the press check where the printer sets up the press using the final film and an approved color proof. A designer or production person then recommends color adjustments and signs off on an approved press sheet. The press sheet is then used to compare sheets throughout the press run to ensure consistency.

APPROPRIATE USES

Use to locate saturation density problems, registration problems, and pixelation of bitmap images. Overlay proofs are an economical way to check the placement of objects, verify that objects overprint and knock out as specified, and confirm that traps print correctly; they are less reliable than laminate proofs for proofing final colors.

Laminate proofs are a commonly used method for color forecasting and for identifying most moiré problems. However, keep in mind that unless the base material for the proof is your paper, the printed colors may still look slightly different.

Digital proofing can achieve high quality and can use the actual paper stock you intend to print on rather than sheets of laminate and acetate. However, most digital proofs do not show moirés and trapping errors. High-end digital proofs are more accurate but costly.

Use bluelines to check for film scratches and smudges, and to verify that all pages are in the correct order, that text and graphics print on the appropriate pages, and that page elements are accurately aligned.

Press proofs are the only way to see the true effects of color on the paper you've selected. Look for misregistration, color shifts, knockouts and overprinted spots, and streaks of errant color. Discuss placement of images if roller marks or other press limitations are apparent.

Checking Color Proofs

Color proofs that you sign off on, sometimes called contract proofs, indicate to the commercial printer the color you expect in the final document. These proofs provide your best way of judging how the colors in your publication will appear when printed.

Remember that some spot colors, varnishes, and metallic inks cannot be represented by color proofs. The proof may not accurately show all the qualities of the final printed piece. If you find problems with the color proofs, work with your prepress service provider to find the best way to solve them.

What to look for on color proofs

- Check color tints to make sure they are accurate and do not look mottled.

- Check that colors are even and consistent throughout the proofs.

- Check "memory" colors, that is, colors that are expected to look a certain way: skin tones, sky, grass, and so on. If these colors are off, the whole piece will be perceived to be incorrect.

- Check colors selected from color-matching systems against printed swatches.

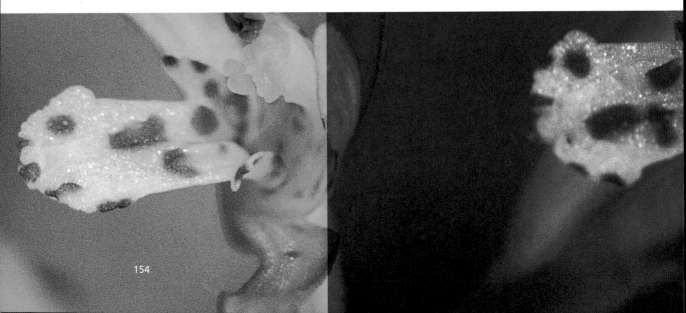

- Check colors selected from color-matching systems against printed swatches.

- Compare the color bars to standard ones. This will show if detail has been lost because of overexposure.

- Look at the trim marks to make sure that bleeds and crossovers extend the required amount beyond the marks.

- Check for type that is too weak or breaking up due to overexposure.

- If images appear flat, look closely at the highlights and shadows. If highlight dots are too large, the whites will appear slightly gray. If the shadow dots are too small, the black will not be strong enough.

- In landscape images, examine clouds to see that the magenta and yellow dots are as small as possible, with cyan dots only slightly bigger. A sky can look dirty because of too much yellow.

Checking Press Proofs

On a press check, plates made from the output film are mounted on a press. The press is prepared with the correct inks and paper, and several tests are run to ensure correct ink coverage and register.

After this process, called *make-ready*, is complete, sheets of your publication are printed and made available for proofing. You, the press operator, and the customer service representative then examine the sheets for final quality.

At this point, concentrate on changes that can be made by adjusting the press, such as color densities or color consistency. If you have a color that you are trying to match, be sure to give it to the printer in advance. It is expensive to make any other changes to your publication beyond press adjustments.

What to look for on the press proof

- Is the type sharp? Use a loupe to look for broken or doubled lines.

- Are the colors and type density consistent from one end of the sheet to the other?

- Is the color correct? Compare the press sheet to the contract proof.

- Is the paper or printed surface the one you specified? Bring a sample with you to compare to the press proof.

- Are crossovers correct? Fold the press page and check the alignment and color match.

- Are halftone dots sharp in the highlights and shadows? Use a loupe to make sure that details and highlights match the contract proof.

- If spot-color inks are used, are they as specified?

- Are there blemishes or mottling of color?

- Check all areas of the press sheet for spots caused by problems with the press.

- Are all graphic elements present? Compare the press sheet to the blueline proof.

- Are separations in register? Check to make sure all separations line up on the register marks. Under a loupe, four-color subjects using traditional screening should show a rosette pattern, and no more than a single line of dots of a single color should be visible at the edge of the image.

- Always take a couple of approved press sheets with you for later reference.

Color Bars

Color bars—those rows of color patches you see on your prepress and press proofs—give proofing and press operators a way to control each step in the production process. Although most color bar elements require sophisticated equipment and training to analyze properly, an understanding of their uses can help you monitor the quality of your print project.

Prepress and print vendors purchase original film or the rights to digital files of color bars and other test images for each job. Because these images do not change from one print job to another, they serve as constant reference points throughout the proofing, plate-making, and press stages.

Color bars are essential troubleshooting tools at the proofing stage because they allow the vendor to evaluate the proof and determine the source of any variance from the expected image quality. They are also easy to analyze, both visually and with a densitometer—an instrument for measuring the relative density of any part of an image.

Digital files or original film of most color bars are supplied by numerous organizations, including E. I. DuPont de Nemours (DuPont), the Graphic Arts Technical Foundation (GATF), and the Rochester Institute of Technology.

Recognizing color bar elements

Essentially, color bars and other test images are made up of small graphics (called patches or elements) of varying shapes, colors, tints, and patterns that are often grouped in rows. Each of the hundreds of elements currently in use by commercial prepress and press houses is designed for a specific purpose. Common color bar elements can be categorized as follows.

Solid-color patch. The most basic element of a test image is the solid-color patch—one for each of the process colors (cyan, magenta, yellow, and black). Solid-color patches are used to measure ink densities, according to industry or the print vendor's standards. Its geometric shape is usually a square and can be measured roughly by sight and precisely with a densitometer.

Tint patch. A tint patch is a solid-color patch whose color is less than 100%. Most color bars include several patches for each process color set at different tint percentages; the de facto standards in the United States are 25%, 50%, and 75% tints. Tint patches permit the measurement of dot gain because they are created by halftone screens. Studies have shown that tint patches correlate more closely with the appearance of a color reproduction than solid patches because fluctuations in dot gain have more impact on color reproduction than solid ink density.

Solid overprint patch. Solid overprint patches show the effects of combining individual solid-color patches. Most color bars include red (magenta and yellow), blue (cyan and magenta), and green (cyan and yellow) solid overprint patches; many also have three- and four-color patches. If a solid overprint patch shows uneven color coverage, it indicates an inking problem on press.

Tint overprint patch. Tint overprint patches combine tint patches of more than one color. Gray-balance tint overprint patches are particularly useful because these neutrals are made up of nearly equal amounts of cyan, magenta, and yellow (there is slightly more cyan than magenta and yellow). An imbalance in any one of these process colors—whether from incorrect ink density or from dot gain—can result in an easily detectable color cast in the patch.

Standard Lighting

If you expect to get predictable results from your color reproduction system, you must consider the lighting where you work and the lighting you use to check proofs.

In a truly professional working environment, you'll find workstations in rooms with no windows; walls painted neutral gray; consistent, color-correct (5000° Kelvin) lighting; monitors calibrated to the final color output; and viewing booths with color-correct lighting.

Since most of us don't have such a workplace, you should try to maintain consistent lighting in your work area. If your computer is near a window, cover the window so that the light on your monitor is as consistent as possible. View proofs in color-correct light. If you have to look at proofs without the benefit of color-correct light, always view all your proofs under the same lighting conditions.

The GATF star target is sensitive to directional characteristics such as *slurring* (when round dots become oval) or halftone dot doubling.

Printing via Web

With Internet technology rapidly transforming how documents are created and distributed, there is a need for widely accepted standards. Adobe PostScript technology has become the global standard for describing to a printer the appearance of a page, including text, graphics, and scanned images. WebReady printing, an optional feature of PostScript 3.0, integrates the printing process with the Internet. This allows you to print from the same medium you increasingly rely on for accessing content. WebReady systems are ideally suited for the intranets within businesses and enterprises.

The WebReady printing option is made up of four components:

- The HTTP server allows you to communicate over the Web among user systems, printer clients, and printer management clients.

- The Web client allows your WebReady printer to pull documents from the Web for printing, just as your system employs a Web browser to download documents.

- The Web job manager maintains and updates your print job status.

- Web file format interpreters and converters interpret Web documents in most file formats or convert them to the PostScript language for printing.

These components of WebReady printing allow you to use the Web efficiently for transmitting files to remote printers and to manage printers over the Web.

earth&ware
★ the gardener's catalog ✦

Purpose &
longevity
separate an
ordinary
gadget
from the
invaluable
tool.

Much like a well-appointed kitchen

a good shed is filled only with

the essentials—

those tools that turn tiresome chores

into simple tasks. with

routine care, all our products

promise a lifetime of use.

boots

shovels

enhance the flavor of your meals with a

selection of herbs from Earth & Ware. While fall is usually reserved for

yard work and preparation for the colder months ahead,

it's also the perfect time to let her plants mature indoors.

sunny kitchen window for a

herb. By spring you'll have

Composite Workflow

Ensuring successful print publishing requires management of every aspect of the workflow—the entire publication process from content creation through printing. One of the most challenging aspects of workflow management is the movement of a job through the workflow—both for reviews and during the prepress and print production process.

Most publications are distributed in the format of the authoring application, or native format. Once approved, the files are saved in PostScript or a proprietary format for prepress work and final printing. Because so many different applications generate PostScript is so many different ways, however, PostScript files may be arbitrarily large and complex. In addition, reliability problems, such as missing fonts, corrupt files, missing graphics elements, and features unsupported by different output processors, result in an industry-wide fail rate of over 50% for first-time print jobs.

Adobe Portable Document Format (PDF) is a highly structured document format based on the PostScript language and developed for seamless portability between computer platforms and output devices. PDF files are created by "distilling" any of the hundreds of varieties of PostScript files into a single, compact format that contains all of the fonts, graphics, and high-end print information

needed to view and print the document. Using Adobe Acrobat, publishers can review, edit, and print any PDF file on Macintosh, Windows, and UNIX platforms.

Today, many large publishers are using PDF to streamline their review and production cycles. For example, numerous magazines and newspapers, including the Associated Press, have adopted PDF as the standard format for delivering ads via satellite or ISDN lines to local publishing offices. PDF enables local publishers to instantly view the ad exactly as designed, make late-stage text edits, and reliably print from any computer.

On the production end, service bureaus are using PDF to build more reliable PostScript language files either for printing directly or to send through the prepress workflow. By distilling a native file and then using Acrobat to save the file back to PostScript, a service bureau can remove much of the arbitrary information introduced by the authoring application and create a more tightly structured and reliable PostScript file. This process is especially useful when the driver used in the creation of the PostScript file doesn't match the configuration of the final output device.

Archiving in PDF

To be useful in the future as a source of images and text, your document should be archived in a format that is likely to remain in widespread use for a long time. Caution is advisable when archiving your document in proprietary formats, or in formats specific to an application. The application may be replaced, sometimes within a surprisingly short period, and it may then be impossible to print from the archive. If you began working with personal computers in 1986, for example, almost every file you completed that year can no longer be opened.

Portable Document Format (PDF) provides a way to store publications in a format that can be viewed and printed with 100% fidelity without the fonts, artwork, and software used to create the publications. Archived PDF files can be opened, printed, and exchanged in any of the common environments, including Macintosh, Windows, and UNIX. Large libraries of PDF files can be indexed and searched, and text and images can be copied into other applications.

Files archived in PDF provide an extractable database of material that can be updated and reused in future publications.

Mount Rainier
Things to do and see

T hroughout the year, you can enjoy numerous park activities and programs, including guided nature walks, cross-country skiing, and snowshoeing. Check the park newspapers for current programs and schedules.

Popular sights:
- Carbon River
- Sunshine Point
- Longmire
- Paradise
- Ohanapecosh

GUSTAVE BAUMANN

BAUMANN WAS BORN IN GERMANY
1909 - 1916. KNOWN AS ONE OF THE WORLD'S
ARTISTS, HE DIED IN SANTA FE.

PERCY MORAN

BORN IN NEW YORK, MORAN STUDIED
HIS WORK IS IN MAJOR MUSEUMS THROUGHOUT THE

PAULINE PALMER

PALMER WORKED IN CHICAGO AND PROVI
RECIPIENT OF MANY NATIONAL AND INTERNATIONAL AW
HER LIFETIME.

CAROLINE COVENTRY HAYNES

HAYNES EXHIBITED HER WORK THE EARL
AT THE NATIONAL ACADEMY OF DESIGN AND BOSTON AR
EMBER OF THE NATIONAL ASSOCIATION OF WOMEN PA

JANE PETERSON

PETERSON WA
LIFETIME. SI

THE ART OF THE GARDEN

166

Mirelez/Ross Inc. used laser proofs and proofs from a color copier to gain client approval for *The Art of the Garden*. Cromalins were produced for color correction and composite color proofs were made of each page to facilitate positioning the art. The prepress service provider color-corrected the scanned images and trapped the files. Mirelez checked page sequence and artwork placement on bluelines.

Mirelez handed off his first electronic file to his prepress service provider—one large PageMaker file stored on a small, portable hard disk. This was a risky proposition for a designer accustomed to delivering layout boards where he could see the exact layout. Mirelez said he also took several other risks in the project, ranging from mixing contemporary computer graphics with traditional paintings to using an untested method of bookbinding.

The Art of the Garden was the first publication Mirelez produced with PageMaker, and he said that the interface made it easy to work in. Mirelez offered this advice to designers using PageMaker: "Get to know the program; explore its capabilities. It does beautiful things."

Print production is an expertise

that most designers

don't take seriously. Good production

techniques will make or

break the design.

–Mary K. Baumann,
Hopkins/Baumann, New York, NY

4

Project Management Guidelines

The publishing process

Pocketbook issues

Reviewing your print quality requirements

Choosing prepress tasks

Selecting vendors

Decisions involving your printer

Tips for working with page-layout files

File handoff checklist

Real-world project

Project Management Guidelines

Every commercial printing job requires that you consider a complex set of variables ranging from what your budget and schedule allow to how the paper stock and printing press affect your final output. The earlier you think about these variables, the more control you'll have over the quality, cost, and schedule of your project.

Preparing a publication for commercial printing takes careful thought: Both imagesetters and commercial printing presses have inherent limitations, and it's possible to create publications that are difficult to print on either an imagesetter or a printing press. By thinking of your design and production cycles as steps in a larger process, you can make choices that will let you work more efficiently and help you achieve the best printed results.

In addition to choosing a commercial printer, you may need to select a prepress service provider. If your printer provides a full range of prepress services, consider having all the work done at one place. One-stop shopping may prevent misunderstanding and improve quality control. Prepress work includes scanning continuous-tone art, imaging color separations, trapping, and imposition. Several types of vendors provide these services: prepress houses, color trade shops, and color-capable imagesetting service bureaus, as well as some commercial printers. Shop for vendors who are willing to answer your printing questions, and ask to see samples of their work.

The Publishing Process

Successfully completing a commercially printed publication requires several steps including planning and organizing, design and content development, and prepress tasks where your electronic files are prepared to be reproduced with ink on paper.

Making informed decisions in the planning stages builds a solid foundation for your project. When you have questions about your project, seek advice from your vendors. Keep track of decisions you make: who is responsible for the completion and quality of each task, when each phase must be completed, and what requirements must be met for the final output.

Choose prepress tasks

Determine which prepress tasks you will do based on your available resources and final schedule. Specialized tasks such as trapping and high-resolution scanning may need to be sent out.

Define project and quality requirements

Before you start to work, gather all the requirements for the publication, including budget, schedule, and output quality.

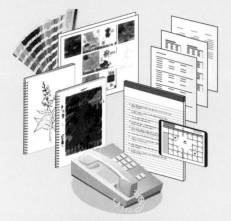

Select and consult your vendors

Evaluate commercial printers and prepress service providers based on the requirements of your project and the services you require. Visit the sites of potential vendors. Select a commercial printer and prepress service provider early in the design process, so that they can assist you in planning.

Create your publication

Define the colors you will use and decide if they will be process or spot colors. Assemble the text, and the vector, raster, and line art for your publication. Review the design to determine how the page elements interact and overlap. Determine if you will use a CMS. Discuss printing issues with your commercial printer as your design evolves.

The Publishing Process *(continued)*

Check the desktop proofs

Print proof copies of your publication on a black-and-white or color PostScript desktop printer. Consult your printer about what proofing methods are recommended to check color quality and to safeguard against production problems.

5

Hand off your files

Decide what type of file to give to your printer or service provider. Gather your files, the final laser proofs, your checklist listing details about your document, and any additional files, such as raster images and vector artwork. Coordinate with whoever will be taking charge at the print shop or service bureau, and turn over the files to them.

6

Check the final proofs and authorize printing

Examine the film separations for quality and accuracy. Check that objects appear on the correct separation. Check proofs made from separations for correct trapping and smooth and consistent tints. Meet with your printer to review press proofs for final color quality. After you approve the press proof, the publication is printed and assembled.

Archive your publication

After your publication has been printed, you need to store all of your files in a consistent manner so that you can quickly find and update them if needed. Decide on what type of media you will use and develop a naming system that will allow you to search for all files needed to reprint your publication.

Pocketbook Issues

Every print project requires you to balance cost, schedule, and quality. When preparing a budget, estimate fixed and variable costs. Fixed costs do not vary depending on how many copies of the job you print. These costs include payment for designing, writing, editing, scanning, and print preparation. Variable costs—those costs that vary depending on how many copies you print—include press time, paper, and binding costs.

Estimate the resources and skills of the workgroup assigned to the project. If you have the expertise and equipment to do some of the prepress work in-house, it can be cheaper than having it done by an outside contractor. But doing your own prepress work can cost more if the work is done incorrectly, since you may not discover mistakes until your publication is imaged on film.

Making changes late in the project cycle can result in missed press dates, additional charges from the printer, and delays in binding and delivery. As a general rule, the closer corrections are made to the press date, the more expensive they will be.

A key factor in determining how much your project will end up costing is how clearly you communicate with whoever is doing prepress work and imaging the files. If you and your service provider understand each other's requirements, you can both take steps to limit costs while ensuring the project's success.

Reviewing Your Requirements

Both the cost and the impact of your publication are greatly affected by the printing process. The cost can also be affected by the requirements of your schedule—a rush job may be more costly than a background job that the printer can run when the press would otherwise be idle. While you want the best quality for your publication, knowing the degree of tolerance you have for a particular project is important for both you and your printer. Asking yourself the following questions may help you arrive at requirements appropriate to your project:

- Audience: How do you need to influence your audience? Does the printed piece have to distinguish itself visually from similar pieces? Does it have to get the attention of an audience to inform them, or is the audience anticipating the information in the piece? Must the piece appeal visually to design-conscious buyers?

- Length of time on the market: Is this a publication that announces a onetime-only offer (like a sale flyer) or will it be used over and over again (like a cookbook)?

- Image issues: Is visual detail important to the message? Illustrations in a history textbook may not be color critical, but the detail must be clear for the image to be informative. Flesh tones should always look human and healthy. Images for a clothing catalog require clear detail, especially for fine prints and textures.

- Color matching: Will people make critical decisions based on the color in the piece? Clothing catalogs usually require an exact match to the actual clothing. If the color is wrong, customers may be dissatisfied with the clothing they receive. In other cases, it's more important for colors to be balanced; food images in grocery ads or cookbooks require a pleasing photograph, but not necessarily a color match.

Sample requirements:

Newsletters

The newsletter is printed with one ink (usually black), photographs are recognizable but may lose some detail from the original, and the paper stock is a standard type always kept on hand. The piece is designed to be read and eventually replaced with the next edition.

Hardware direct-mail catalog

The catalog is printed using paper and inks regularly kept in stock by the printer. The standard size makes it cheaper to bind and finish. The catalog includes crisp black-and-white photographs and color photographs with good detail. Color accuracy is important but not critical because buying decisions are not usually based on the represented color. Registration is accurate to 1/100 inch. The publication will be replaced in several months.

High-end clothing catalog

The high-end catalog uses premium papers and inks. Color in the photographs is required to match the actual clothing. Printer registration is very accurate, and all the artwork is trapped. Although the expected duration of the publication is short, a high-quality publication helps persuade the audience to buy.

Fortune 500 corporate annual report

In an annual report, the image of the company is conveyed by the quality of design, printing, and appearance of the publication. Color, while less critical than in a clothing catalog, is accurate and black-and-white photographs are very sharp. The product has no discernible flaws.

Choosing Prepress Tasks

Scanning and color correction

 One of the most difficult decisions regarding a project is how much of the prepress work you will do from the desktop. With the expanding range of desktop publishing tools, the temptation is to do many of the tasks yourself. But tasks that can be done on the desktop require skill, time, and equipment you may not have or want to acquire.

**Color separation
Trapping
Digital screening**

A decision critical to the final stage concerns the format in which you hand off your files. You may choose to turn over files in their native format and let the vendor convert them to PostScript for imaging onto film. In that case, you hand over files in the formats appropriate to your page-layout, illustrator, or image-editing programs, and the vendor converts them. Or you may choose to do the conversion to PostScript yourself.

Your relationship with your printer can affect your decision on which prepress tasks you do. If you intend to exercise a large amount of control over the publication, and assume the responsibility for the quality of the film, you may choose to do all the prepress work yourself and deliver a final PostScript file to your prepress service provider for imaging. If you want your service provider to be able to make changes to your publication, discuss this with your service provider and hand off your files in the agreed-on form.

Converting files to PostScript for imaging

The following table is intended to help weigh the trade-offs in choosing prepress tasks.

WHAT YOU NEED

You can scan images using a flatbed or transparency scanner. Scanned images can be large and require large amounts of disk storage. Your computer needs a fast processor and plenty of RAM. To adjust color, you need image-editing software, such as Adobe Photoshop.

It is likely that several of the desktop tools you are already using—such as illustration, image-editing, and page-layout programs—can generate color separation files, do trapping automatically, and generate halftone screens in raster form.

For example, with a program like Adobe Illustrator you can separate and trap color artwork before it is imported into PageMaker.

When preparing a PostScript file, you must use the correct PostScript Printer Description (PPD) for the output device. Document files must be linked. Your fonts must be available on the host computer. Print settings must be correct. You should be able to interpret and respond to error messages.

WHAT VENDORS CAN DO

A prepress service provider can use a high-end drum scanner that provides superior image quality. Along with the large, high-resolution files, low-resolution versions can be provided to speed up design and proofing.

Prepress service providers often use dedicated trapping software, to trap publications with superior results. High-end proprietary color-separation systems also provide trapping.

Prepress professionals already know what range of registration error to expect from the press where your job will be printed, so they know how much trapping is needed.

When generating halftone screens they already know how much to allow for dot gain.

Service providers usually know what to look for to ensure that files will image properly. If you hand off a file in the format of your layout program, the service provider can adjust settings and make whatever corrections are needed to get your file onto film.

TRADE-OFFS

Doing your own image editing can be time-consuming, but you have complete control over the appearance of the final image.

High-end drum scanning is costly, but you may need the superior resolution and color correction that it provides.

Automatic trapping tools eliminate some of the need for specialized knowledge but may not be able to trap all the elements in your publication.

If you do the trapping yourself you need to know where traps are necessary, and to find out from your commercial printer what the probable range of registration error will be.

If you do the screening yourself, you must find out from your printer the dot gain to expect with the press and paper being used, so you can correct for dot gain.

When handing off a PostScript file, you have control and responsibility over settings selected in the file and little margin for error. When you hand off prior to converting to PostScript, you relinquish some control to your service provider but leave more leeway for problems to be corrected.

Selecting Vendors

If you don't already have a printer, you may want to consult local design firms about which printers they use. Examine printed material that is similar to your project and find out who printed it. Decide if you want to work with a commercial printer who does the prepress work in-house, or if you prefer to have prepress work done at a different location. Obtaining prepress services from a commercial printer allows you to communicate with only one vendor and manage only one relationship. If you choose to work with several vendors, make sure they understand each other's requirements.

Regardless of whether you are considering having the prepress work be done in-house at the printer's or at a separate shop, there are some questions to raise that relate specifically to prepress work and some that relate to printing.

Questions to ask about prepress services

- What type of imagesetters are available?

- How often are their imagesetters calibrated? Knowledgeable facilities calibrate both daily and every time the film is changed.

- What screening and proofing options are available and how many proofing cycles are permitted? Is the recommended proofing option calibrated to the final output device?

- What file formats do they accept? From which platforms? Do they offer OPI architecture?

- Do they offer scanning?

- If you have already chosen particular fonts, are those you selected available?

- Do they trap manually only, or use trapping software as well?

- What Postscript Printer Description (PPD) should be used in preparing files?

- Do they support color management using ICC profiles? Can their scanner generate a tagged scan? Can they provide an ICC profile for output devices/separation tables?

Questions to ask about printing

- Are both sheet-fed and web-fed presses available? The former are fed individual sheets of paper, print more slowly, and tend to be used for smaller jobs. The latter are fed from a continuous roll, print faster (tens of thousands of impressions per hour), and are used for large jobs. The nature of your job determines which is preferable.

- How many colors can be printed in one press run? On a two-color press, your four-color job will require two press runs. You may be able to cut costs by shopping for a commercial printer with a four-color press.

- If you need high-fidelity color printing, do they do it? This refers to advanced processes that achieve more vibrant color and eliminate the risk of getting moiré patterns.

- What are the options for handling imposition? Can they do it electronically? Will they accept sheets of film with the pages already imposed?

- What color-matching systems are supported? Photoshop, Illustrator, and PageMaker support several spot and process color-matching systems including ones made by PANTONE, TruMatch, and Focoltone.

Decisions Involving Your Printer

Once you have made a choice, discuss specifics of the project with your printer. You may wish to inquire about:

- The appropriate screen ruling (lpi) to use

- The dot gain from film to press

- The trap specifications for your job

- Any other recommended settings to use

The printer may have recommendations related to your design and choice of color. Having the right paper stock, coating, and ink types can be important to the quality of your final publication, and the availability of critical materials can affect scheduling. You may wish to bring up some of the following topics:

- Your project schedule and budget

- The dimensions of your publication and how many copies you plant to print

- The colors you plan to specify

- Decisions about finishing and binding

- Your use of bleeds and crossovers

- The graphics in your publication

Your printer may have recommendations concerning materials, bindings, or special inks, and may be able to point out ways to save money by making minor changes in your publication. Discussing the project gives the printer a chance to notice if particular inks and grades of paper need to be ordered in advance.

Tips for Working with Page-Layout Files

Generally speaking, these suggestions apply to creating documents in any page-layout program. Some may also be applicable if you are designing individual pages in an illustrator program.

Maintain a clean computer environment. Over time, changes occur to software and hardware that can lead to performance loss and system problems. Defragmenting the hard drive, removing older versions of software, updating device drivers, optimizing memory, and performing other routine maintenance tasks prevents applications and files from becoming damaged.

Create a project folder. Before you begin a project, create a folder in which to store your publication and its linked files, such as images and fonts.

Specify the target resolution. Specify the resolution of your target output device in your page-layout program before you place raster images.

Use a template if available. Use a template if you frequently create similar projects. Templates let you create consistent publications more quickly, while protecting the original file.

Open the publication from the hard drive. Before you open a publication stored on removable media (e.g., floppy disk, Zip disk) or a network drive, copy it to your hard drive. The slower access time between the hard drive and the removable or network drive can cause data to become incomplete, lost, or corrupt, resulting in damage to your publication.

Maintain a backup copy. System errors can happen unexpectedly. To prevent losing your work if an error occurs while you're in a publication, always create a backup copy of the publication and update it frequently.

Save your publication frequently. Save your publication immediately after you create it. Then, save it again each time you make changes that would be difficult or time-consuming to re-create. In the event of a power failure or system error, saving your publication frequently ensures you won't lose many changes.

If possible use a widely supported class of fonts. Not all imaging and printing devices employ the same format for representing fonts. To be safe, check that the class of fonts you are using is supported by the system that will ultimately rasterize and image your text.

Graphic format. Most software applications support a variety of graphic file formats. Make sure the format you are using is compatible with the system doing the final imaging.

Place graphics rather than copying and pasting them. Having graphics linked to places in the text, rather than pasted in, makes efficient use of time and computer resources. A document with rasterized illustrations pasted directly into the text is generally cumbersome and can take a long time to save.

Verify your links are intact before printing. To ensure your publication prints correctly, verify all your links are intact. This is especially important if you've stored graphics outside the publication.

File Handoff Checklist

You may be able to minimize surprises and surcharges from your prepress vendor by using the following checklist when preparing your files for handoff. See "Including a Report" on pages 146-147 for a sample service provider report.

☐ **Create a label.** If your application doesn't provide automatic labels, create a label in your file that will print at least the filename and date.

☐ **Eliminate unnecessary elements.** Delete all extraneous colors, patterns, and other elements from the file, including those that may be invisible or behind other elements or layers.

☐ **Use the correct format.** Make sure all files are in the correct format. Consult your prepress vendor for the best format to use.

☐ **Set halftone screens correctly.** If you plan to place Adobe Photoshop images saved in EPS format in a page-layout document, select your halftone screen frequency in the page-layout program rather than in each image. If any image screen frequency conflicts with that of the page-layout application, the image setting may override that of the document, often with poor results.

☐ **Size, rotate, and crop to final dimensions.** As much as possible, provide correctly sized art in the correct rotated position to the prepress vendor. Provide a clipping path in the raster image, where possible. Sizing, cropping, and rotating raster images in a page-layout application are very complex operations; as a result, the raster image processor (RIP) may take a long time to process the file.

☐ **Make spot colors consistent.** If you use the same spot color and tint several times in one document, be consistent in specifying each object's custom color and tint. If you want the vendor to convert certain custom colors to process colors, indicate where you want that done.

☐ **Record separation settings.** As you work with each image (not after the fact), record the settings used. In Adobe Photoshop use the File Info command to record the separation settings you used when converting your image to CMYK. To print this information when proofing your image, use the Captions attribute in File Info, then check the Caption box in the Page Setup dialog box.

☐ **Provide laser prints.** Print your files first on a PostScript laser printer. Send laser prints with your files, so the prepress vendor can check against them—making sure the prints are identical to the files in every respect: size, content, placement, bleeds, crops, traps, and so forth. If providing a desktop color composite for the printer to refer to, consider using a CMS to get as accurate a rendering of color as possible. If predictable color is critical to the project, consider investing in a contract color proof.

☐ **Group graphics and document files.** Copy all of the graphics required for your files and place them in the same folder or directory as the page layout or other output files. Make sure the same versions of all images are linked to their correct placements in the document.

☐ **Provide contact information.** In a work order or cover letter, list your name, company name, and contact names and phone numbers, including after-hours numbers, if applicable. Include document specifications. List each filename, document page size, number of pages, which pages to print from each file, and the type of output you need.

☐ **Identify your film requirements.** For each output file, indicate whether you want a positive or negative, the emulsion direction, and the screen frequency for film output.

☐ **List font filenames.** Provide the precise filenames and manufacturers of every typestyle of every font used in your document, as well as whether each is a Type 1 or TrueType font.

☐ **Indicate your trapping needs.** For color separations, indicate whether you've created trapping yourself or want the prepress vendor to do it (usually for a fee).

"

Careful planning is the best defense

against unexpected problems.

Test everything early in production—

fonts, scanned art, EPS graphics, etc.—

when mistakes are cheaper

and easier to fix. Make a thorough

checklist and follow it religiously.

Then pray.

–Eric & Jan Martí, Command Z, Palo Alto, CA

"

BECAUSE *THE ART OF THE GARDEN* features reproductions of artwork for sale, the quality of the paper stock was very important. For the inside pages, Mirelez chose a premium paper stock that was natural in color and very smooth to the touch. This was contrasted by his selection of an industrial-type uncoated paper stock for the cover and a rough, heavy card stock for the binding.

Mirelez chose to work with a prepress service provider recommended by his client. Mirelez worked very closely with the service provider to make sure that details were handled correctly. The prepress service provider scanned 4-by-5-inch transparencies of the gallery artwork on a Scitex scanner. The other graphics were scanned using a desktop scanner, imported into Adobe Photoshop for retouching and manipulation, and then placed in PageMaker. The scanned art was printed at a very fine screen ruling (200 lpi) to capture the detail.

Mirelez works with several commercial printers. He chooses the commercial printer based on the requirements of the job. For example, he may work with one commercial printer for a two-color job and a different one for a four-color process job. According to Mirelez, a good rapport with his printers ensures the success of the projects.

Appendix A: PostScript Errors

PostScript Errors

When you send a page file to a PostScript printer, the first thing that happens is that the file gets rasterized: put in a form understandable by the printer engine. The printer contains a PostScript interpreter capable of translating PostScript files into corresponding raster images, which govern the print mechanism and so are transferred to paper.

Something similar happens when a file is imaged on film for commercial printing. The incoming file is first rasterized by a PostScript interpreter, which in this context is called the Raster Image Processor (RIP).

In either case, if there is something wrong with the original file's PostScript code, the interpreter will detect an error—a PostScript error. When such an error occurs, the interpreter executes special code, called an error handler, designed to address that particular error. The error handler records information in the RIP's memory about the error and then executes a command to stop processing the file.

At this point, the PostScript code in the file may ignore the command to stop processing so that the interpreter may continue executing the file. For example, a file's request for duplex (two-sided) printing on paper will likely cause an error if it's sent to a printer that prints on only one side of the paper. If so, the internal error handler for that error executes the command to stop the job. But the PostScript file may ignore the command to stop as well as the request for duplex printing (the source of the error). Although the job will not fail in this case, it will print only single-sided pages. If the PostScript code does not ignore the command to stop, the interpreter processes the informa-

tion recorded earlier by the internal error handler, which usually produces a message that looks like this:

%%[Error: <error name>; OffendingCommand: <command name>]%%

%%[Flushing: rest of job (to end-of-file) will be ignored]%%

The first line shows the name of the error as well as the name of the PostScript command that caused the error. The second line states that the rest of the job will not be processed. (This particular error message is very useful, although you may not always be able to see it.) The interpreter will then stop executing the file.

The RIP may create other error messages that look like the one shown above. If the messages have a similar format but do not contain the words Error and OffendingCommand, however, they are very likely not PostScript errors. For example, you may see a message containing the label PrinterError, such as:

%%[PrinterError: Media jam]%%

This type of message does not represent an error in the PostScript file detected by the interpreter. It represents a different type of problem that was detected by some other part of the system, in this case by the printer engine.

PostScript Errors *(continued)*

An error message may give little indication of what to do to correct the error. Suppose you encounter this message:

%%[Error: limitcheck;
OffendingCommand: sethalftone]%%

This gives notice that an error called limitcheck occurred when a command called sethalftone was executed in the file, but doesn't reveal much about the source of the problem. In some cases, you may get a clue from the name of the error or command involved. In this example, you might guess that the error was produced by some limit that was reached while attempting to set up a halftone screen. You can make more educated guesses by consulting the *PostScript Language Reference Manual*, or by using the next two tables.

The first table provides a list of operators that can occur as offending commands. The second table lists errors and what to do about them. Analyzing an error message may involve looking up the offending command to determine what type of operation failed as well as determining what type of failure occurred.

TABLE 1: POSTSCRIPT OPERATORS

Operator Category	Category Description	Sample Operators	Operator Descriptions
Graphics State, Device-Independent	Used to control how objects are painted; results should not vary from one type of output-device engine to another.	**setcolor** **setlinewidth**	Establishes the color for an object to be painted. Establishes the thickness of painted lines.
Graphics State, Device-Dependent	Used to control how objects are painted; results usually vary from one type of output-device engine to another.	**sethalftone** **setflat**	Establishes a requested halftone screen. Establishes the flatness of curves.
Path Construction	Used to create graphics such as polygons and curves.	**lineto** **curveto** **arc**	Draws a line. Draws a curve. Draws part or all of a circle.
Painting	Used to paint graphics and images.	**stroke** **fill** **image**	Paints the outline of graphics. Paints the interior of graphics. Paints images.
Form and Pattern	Used to generate repeatable forms and patterns.	**setpattern** **execform**	Establishes a pattern. Paints a form.
Device Setup	Used to set up printing attributes.	**setpagedevice**	Installs requested device features.
Character and Font	Used to manipulate fonts and parts of fonts, such as characters.	**findfont** **show**	Looks for and loads a requested font. Paints a character or group of characters.

TABLE 2: POSTSCRIPT ERROR MESSAGES

Error Name	Usual Meaning	Common Problems and Solutions
<fontname> **not found, using Courier.**	The requested font was not supplied by the RIP or was not within the PostScript file. (This error message is formatted differently; it has no offending command.)	Download the missing font to the RIP, include it in the document, or choose a different font.
configurationerror	A requested feature setting cannot be satisfied; often accompanied by an extra **ErrorInfo** field in the error message indicating the requested feature.	Do not request the feature from the printer driver, use a different printer support file, or configure the RIP to support the feature.
dictfull	There is no more room in PostScript data structures called dictionaries; this problem is more common with PostScript Level 1 than with Level 2.	These operators store objects in dictionaries; error requires advanced debugging.
invalidaccess	An attempt was made to put an object into a read-only data structure.	These operators store objects in various PostScript data structures; error requires advanced debugging.
invalidfont	There was an attempt to install a malformed or an improperly licensed font in the RIP's memory.	Replace or reinstall the font on the RIP and/or computer.
invalidrestore	There is a programming problem with memory management.	There is likely a problem with the printer driver; requires advanced debugging.
ioerror	An input/output error occurred while the RIP was processing a file; the file in question could be the actual job or another file referenced by the job file.	The amount of data supplied is incorrect; scan, edit, or import the image again. These characters may indicate a problem with the communications link; move or replace the communications line, check communications settings, disable spoolers, or run the job again.
limitcheck	An implementation or memory limit has been exceeded often because the file or file elements are too large or complex.	A graphic is too complex (this occurs very rarely when using PostScript Level 2). Increase flatness, split paths, simplify the graphic, or lower the printer engine's resolution. The internal representation of the requested halftone screen is too large or too small; consult your RIP vendor. The image is too large, its resolution is too high, or it cannot be rotated. Reduce the size or resolution, rotate the image at a different angle, or rotate it in an image-editing application such as Adobe Photoshop.

Error Name	Usual Meaning	Common Problems and Solutions
rangecheck	A value provided to the operator was outside the acceptable range.	The requested paper tray does not exist; request a different tray from the printer driver. Requires advanced debugging.
stackoverflow	This is a programming problem concerning the filling up of an internal data structure called the operand stack.	May indicate a printer driver problem or interference from a separate utility; requires advanced debugging.
stackunderflow	The operator expected one or more values to be available on the operand stack, but there were none.	May indicate a printer driver problem or interference from a separate utility; requires advanced debugging.
timeout	A time limit for an operation has been exceeded.	A time-out threshold is set too low or there is a communications problem. Use administration software or the printer driver to reset the time-out value on the RIP, or try a different driver.
typecheck	The operator expected a certain type of value on the operand stack, but the wrong type was provided instead.	May be a printer driver problem or interference from a separate utility; requires advanced debugging. This could indicate a problem with the communications link or with the left-over data in the job; try a different communications line or printer driver. This problem may also occur if a PostScript file is saved, transferred to a different computer platform, and downloaded from that computer; try saving the file in ASCII or Text Only rather than binary format.
undefined	The name specified in the OffendingCommand is not known to the RIP.	This is not a PostScript operator; it indicates that the required PostScript code has not been included in a PostScript file saved on the Macintosh. Resave the file. The job contains a nonstandard operator that is not recognized by the RIP; check the driver settings or select a different printer support file. Too much data for an image may have been supplied; scan, edit, or import the image again.
VMerror	The RIP has run out of PostScript virtual memory (VM) during the job.	Reboot the RIP to clear its memory; this error should be very rare when using PostScript Level 2.

Appendix B: Process Color Charts

Process Color Charts

These charts provide a condensed reference for CMYK color combinations. They show the colors resulting from all possible combinations of the four inks at 10, 20, 40, 60, 80, and 100% levels. More extensive charts, covering finer gradations, are available from printers.

Process Color Tints

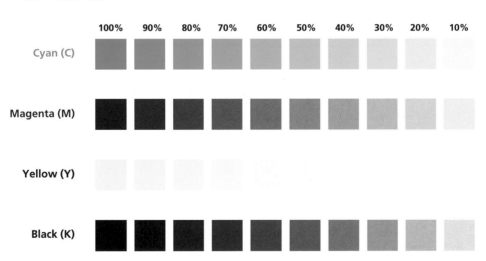

Process Color Mixes: Two-Color Combinations

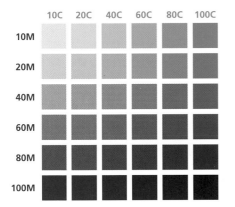

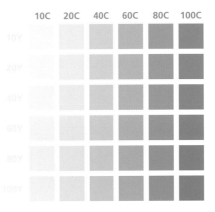

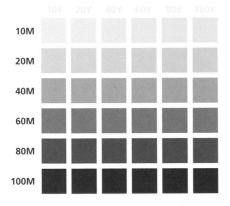

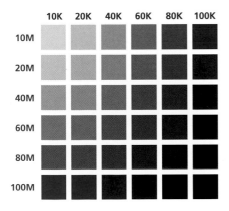

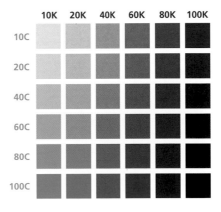

Process Color Mixes: Three-Color Combinations

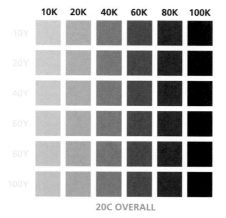

20C OVERALL

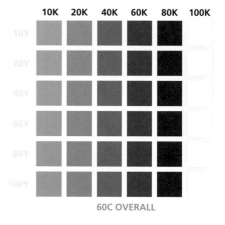

60C OVERALL

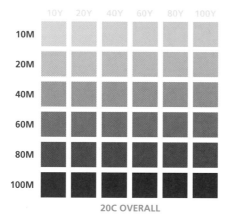

20C OVERALL

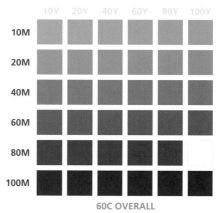

60C OVERALL

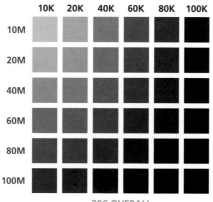

20C OVERALL

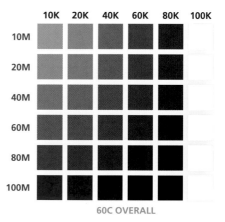

60C OVERALL

Process Color Mixes: Three-Color Combinations

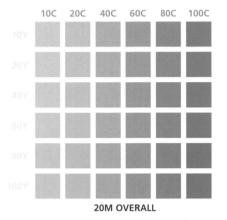

20M OVERALL

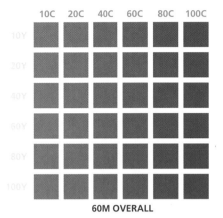

60M OVERALL

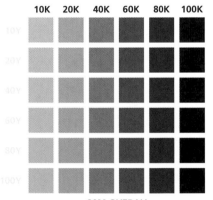

20M OVERALL

60M OVERALL

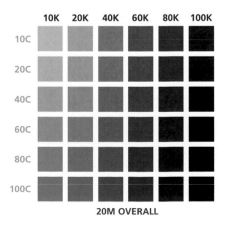

20M OVERALL

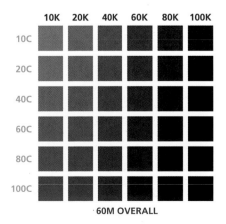

60M OVERALL

Process Color Mixes: Three-Color Combinations

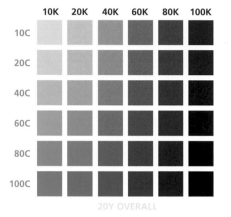

	10K	20K	40K	60K	80K	100K
10C						
20C						
40C						
60C						
80C						
100C						

20Y OVERALL

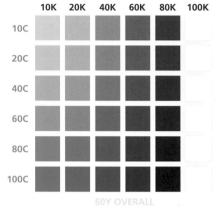

	10K	20K	40K	60K	80K	100K
10C						
20C						
40C						
60C						
80C						
100C						

60Y OVERALL

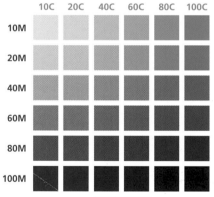

	10C	20C	40C	60C	80C	100C
10M						
20M						
40M						
60M						
80M						
100M						

20Y OVERALL

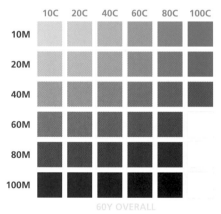

	10C	20C	40C	60C	80C	100C
10M						
20M						
40M						
60M						
80M						
100M						

60Y OVERALL

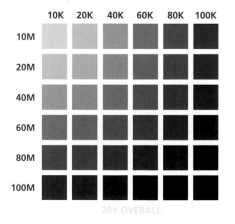

	10K	20K	40K	60K	80K	100K
10M						
20M						
40M						
60M						
80M						
100M						

20Y OVERALL

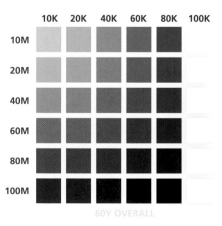

	10K	20K	40K	60K	80K	100K
10M						
20M						
40M						
60M						
80M						
100M						

60Y OVERALL

Process Color Mixes: Three-Color Combinations

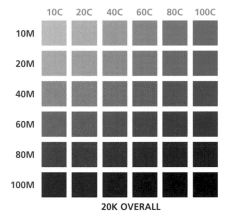

20K OVERALL

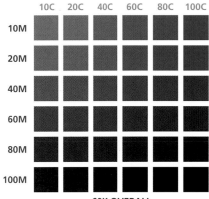

60K OVERALL

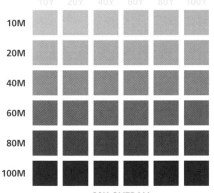

20K OVERALL

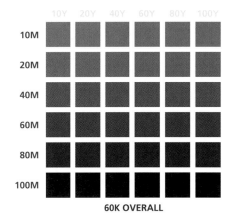

60K OVERALL

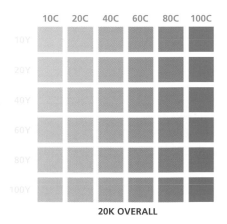

20K OVERALL

60K OVERALL

Process Color Mixes: Four-Color Combinations

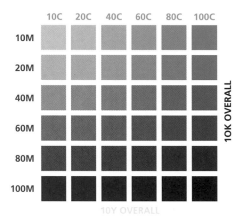

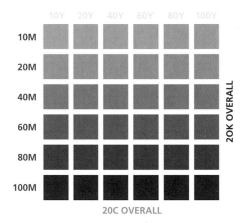

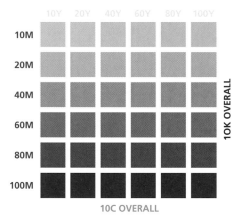

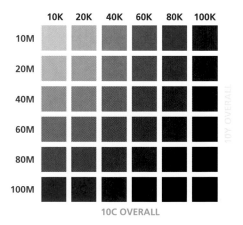

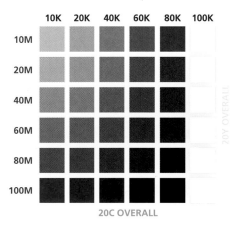

Process Color Mixes: Four-Color Combinations

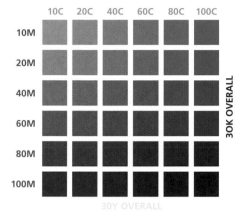

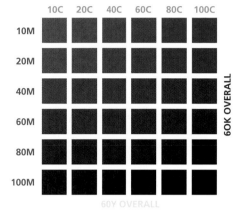

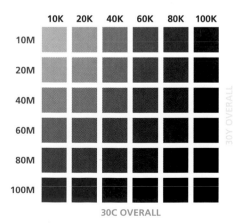

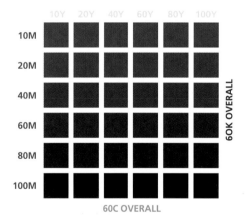

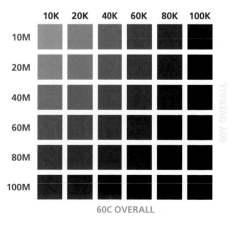

Process Color Mixes: Four-Color Combinations

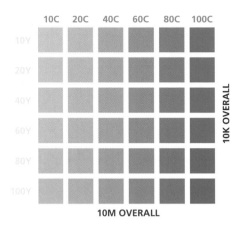

10C 20C 40C 60C 80C 100C
10Y 20Y 40Y 60Y 80Y 100Y
10K OVERALL
10M OVERALL

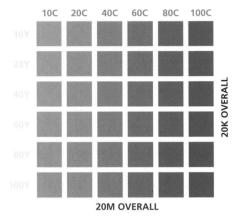

10C 20C 40C 60C 80C 100C
10Y 20Y 40Y 60Y 80Y 100Y
20K OVERALL
20M OVERALL

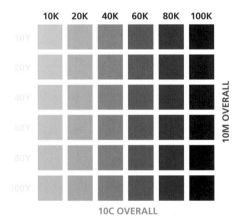

10K 20K 40K 60K 80K 100K
10Y 20Y 40Y 60Y 80Y 100Y
10M OVERALL
10C OVERALL

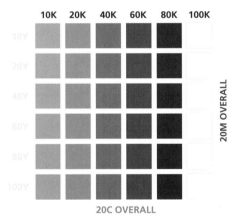

10K 20K 40K 60K 80K 100K
10Y 20Y 40Y 60Y 80Y 100Y
20M OVERALL
20C OVERALL

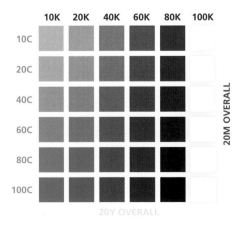

10K 20K 40K 60K 80K 100K
10C 20C 40C 60C 80C 100C
10M OVERALL
10Y OVERALL

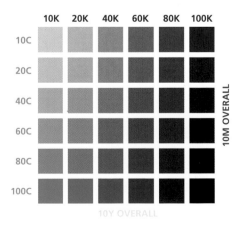

10K 20K 40K 60K 80K 100K
10C 20C 40C 60C 80C 100C
20M OVERALL
20Y OVERALL

Process Color Mixes: Four-Color Combinations

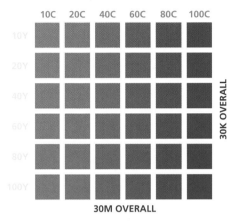

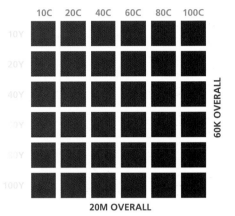

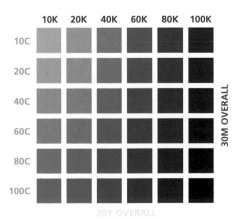

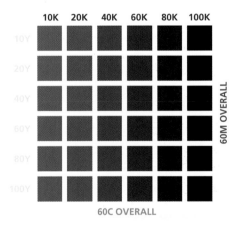

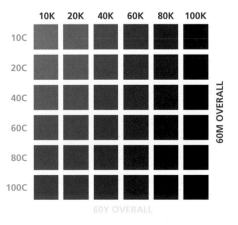

Glossary

accordion fold

Parallel folds, alternating in direction. Also called *concertina fold*.

additive mixing of color

Occurs when two colors of light stimulate the same patch of retina. In commercial color printing, the halftone dots and the overlaps between them together comprise only six colors, plus black. The sensation of full color on a page results from additive mixture of these six colors. *See* secondary color.

alignment

The positioning of text within margins. Text flush with the margins on both sides is referred to as justified. Text is often aligned with only one margin, either the left or the right, and is then described as right/left justified or as ragged left/right.

anchor point

A key element in vector graphics. Curves can be defined, for example, by using the mouse to select anchor points and directions. Pieces of an image can be selected and moved around by moving anchor points. *See* Bezier curve *and* vector graphics.

ascender

The part of lowercase letters (such as k, b, and d) that ascends above the x-height of the other lowercase letters in a typeface.

backslant

A typeface with a backwards slant, the opposite of italic.

baseline

The imaginary line on which the majority of the characters in a typeface rest.

Bezier curve, Bezier surface

Interactive design tools based on formulas developed by Pierre Bezier. A curve or surface is defined by specifying "control points," and manipulated on-screen by moving these points. First used in 1972, for designing automobile bodies.

binding

A process used to assemble pages or signatures.

blanket

In offset printing, a rubber surface that transfers the inked image from plate to paper.

blanket cylinder

In offset presses, the metal cylinder around which the blanket is wrapped.

blind embossing

Uninked letters or patterns appearing in relief.

blueline or blueprint

A photoprint made to proof pagination, image position, and type.

body copy

The text making up the bulk of a document, as distinct from titles and headings. Ordinarily set in 10- or 12-point type, but this can vary either way by as much as 4 points.

boldface

A typeface rendered in darker, thicker strokes so that it will stand out. Boldface is used for emphasis in headlines, while italics are used for emphasis in body text, as a rule.

bullet

A dot or other special character used to indicate items in a list.

butt

Two art elements or colored regions are said to butt if they meet edge to edge.

caliper

The thickness of paper, usually expressed in thousandths of an inch. Also called *bulk*.

camera ready

Said of text or artwork ready to be photographed by a process camera.

cap height

The height from the baseline to the top of the uppercase letters in a font. This may or may not be the same as the height of ascenders. Cap height is used in some systems to measure the type size.

centered text

Text placed at an equal distance from the left and right margins. Headlines are often centered.

Glossary *(continued)*

character

In typography, a single element such as a letter, numeral, or mark of punctuation. Another word for typographic element is *glyph*. In computing, characters are often identified with eight-bit alphanumeric codes. The character code 97, for example, represents the letter *a*.

character encoding

An encoding is a table that maps (usually eight-bit) character codes to the glyphs of a font. There are only 256 possible eight-bit codes, so most computer fonts are limited to that many glyphs. Some fonts, particularly for non-Latin alphabets, use sixteen-bit codes and can therefore contain many more glyphs.

CMYK

The usual abbreviation for cyan, magenta, yellow, and black: the inks used in color process printing. In interactive computer graphics, CMYK is one of the modes used to specify color—essentially by choosing a level for each of the four component inks.

cold-set ink

Molten ink applied with a hot press and solidifying on the paper.

collate

To gather pages in a particular order for binding.

color filter

A sheet of colored glass, plastic, or gelatin with biased transparency. A red filter, for example, lets only red light pass through and absorbs light of other wavelengths. Filters are basic to color scanning and color-separation photography.

color-matching system

Systems based on numbered color samples that allow a designer to specify colors by number.

color separation

Separating a multicolor image into monochrome components. Often done photographically using filters. The result is then typically four sheets of film called "separations," one for each of the CMYK process colors. Separation can also be done digitally, and the corresponding result is a four-part image file.

color sequence

The order in which process colors are printed. A common color sequence is yellow, magenta, cyan, and black.

color value

The tonal value of a color, analogous to gray level on a scale from dark to light.

comprehensive, comp

An accurate layout with text and art positioned as they will appear in the end product.

condensed font

A narrower version of a font, used to get more characters into a given space.

connected dots

Halftone dots connected with their neighbors, which means all dots over the 50% size.

continuous-tone art

Artwork containing tonal gradation, as distinct from solid lines against a blank background. Photographs exemplify continuous-tone art.

contrast

A feature of the grayscale, or more generally of the tonal range. A high-contrast photographic print emphasizes the extremes—very dark and very light areas predominate. A low-contrast print emphasizes the mid-range. In typography, the term is used to describe fonts, referring to variety in line thickness. *See* font contrast.

copyfitting

A typographic process of adjusting the size and spacing of type to make it fit within a defined area or on a definite number of printed pages. Can be done by calculation based on experience, or by successive adjustments at the computer until a fit is reached.

cover stock

Heavyweight paper used for the covers of magazines and booklets.

cropping, crop marks

The trimming, or cropping, of artwork can be done either manually or digitally with an image-editor. Crop marks are marks made on a photograph or other artwork indicating what part to exclude and how the designer wants the image framed.

crossover

Occurs when a graphic element carries over from a page to the one facing it.

curing

Preparing paper for printing by letting it reach the same temperature and humidity levels as the press room.

dampening

In conventional lithography, fountain solution is applied to the plate. Image areas intended for ink have been treated to make them repel the solution. Non-image areas have not been treated and dampening wets them. The inks used will adhere only to dry areas, so dampening serves to confine the ink and define the image.

deckle edge

The naturally ragged edge of untrimmed paper. In some cases the natural edge may be specified by the designer.

densitometer

A device to measure the density of printed color.

Glossary *(continued)*

descender

The part of a lowercase letter (such as y, p, and q) that descends below the baseline. In some typefaces, the uppercase J and Q also descend below the baseline.

die

A stamping tool used in embossing and cutting.

digital graphic effects

Special graphic effects produced with an image-editor or any other tool for modifying raster images. An example is digital posterization: producing areas of uniform color in an image by mathematically reducing the tonal range of each color to a few large steps.

dimensional stability

Paper's resistance to stretching and the like, especially when damp.

dingbats

Nonalphanumeric glyphs. Dingbat fonts consisting entirely of these characters are a source of graphic symbols—such as arrows, bullets, and dividers—and of graphic ornaments.

direct color process

Color separation and screening in a single photographic step. The original is separated, typically into four component monochrome images, and each image is simultaneously resolved into dots. This is in contrast to the indirect color process, which does separation and screening in separate stages.

display type

Type larger than that of the main text, used for headlining and display.

dot-for-dot reproduction

A method of reproducing printed halftone material. Because it has already been resolved into halftone dots, this material is difficult to rescreen. The dot-for-dot method is an alternative that avoids rescreening by duplicating the original's halftone dots.

dot gain

The spread of dots during several stages of printing or platemaking, as measured by the increase in size of a midtone dot. If, for some reason such as paper absorbency, or poor film contact during platemaking, a 50% dot expands into a 60% dot, the gain is 10%.

dpi

An abbreviation for dots per inch. Refers to the resolution at which a device, such as a monitor or printer, can display text and graphics.

drop cap

A document style in which the first capital letter of a paragraph is set in a larger point size and aligned with the top of the first line. Used to indicate the start of a new section of text, such as a chapter.

dry litho or waterless printing

A type of lithographic plate with a coating able to repel ink without needing to be dampened. Ink is confined to the image area without the usual wetting.

drying oven

An oven used to dry paper after printing. In web-fed lithography, the damp paper passes continuously from the press and through the drying oven.

duplex stock

Paper with its two sides colored or finished differently.

ellipsis

A punctuation character consisting of three dots, or periods, in a row. It indicates that a word or phrase has been omitted. To access the ellipsis character in standard typefaces, press Option + semicolon.

elliptical halftone dots

Elongated halftone dots used to improve the tonal mid-range. Resolution into elliptical dots can be done photographically by means of a special screen.

embossing

Producing a raised image in paper by means of a die striking from the back of the paper into a recessed counter die at the front.

em, em space, em quad

A common unit of measurement in typography. The em is traditionally the width of the uppercase M in whatever font is being used. It defines the font's point size. For example, in 12-point type, one em is a distance of 12 points.

em dash

A dash the length of an em is used to indicate a break in a sentence.

en, en space, en quad

A common unit of measurement in typography. Traditionally, the en is the width of the uppercase N in the typeface and point size being used. Technically, it is defined as half the width of an em.

en dash

A dash the length of an en is used to indicate a range of values.

endpapers

The heavy paper at the front and back of a book, to which coverboard is glued.

feathering

A printing problem involving rough or feathered edges.

filling in

A printing problem that occurs when ink fills in letters and the open spaces between halftone dots.

Glossary *(continued)*

flexography

Relief printing using a flexible rubber printing surface. The image is raised above the rest of the surface, as with an ordinary letterpress. Flexography allows printing on curved objects such as beer cans.

flush cover

A book cover that is trimmed flush with the pages of text.

flush left ragged right

Text that is aligned on the left margin is said to be flush left. If the text is unaligned on the right, so that it has a ragged edge, it is said to be flush left ragged right. The term ragged right is sometimes used alone to mean the same thing.

flush right ragged left

Text that is aligned on the right margin is said to be flush right and, if unaligned on the left, is said to be set flush right ragged left. The term ragged left is sometimes used alone to mean the same thing.

font

One style, weight, and width of a typeface. An example is Times roman bold extended. Times is a typeface family, roman is a style, bold is a weight, extended is a width. The terms font and typeface tend to be used interchangeably.

font contrast

Font contrast refers to the range of thickness of the strokes used to draw a font's characters. Helvetica has low contrast, for example, because the letters are drawn with strokes of uniform thickness. Bodoni, on the other hand, has high contrast.

font family

Also called a *typeface family*. A collection of similar fonts designed to be used together. The Garamond family, for example, includes roman and italic styles, several weights (regular, semibold, and bold), and several widths (extended and compressed).

fountain

The supply of ink for a lithographic press. Sometimes also the supply of dampening solution.

galley proof

A proof that is close enough to final copy to permit proofreading. The traditional galley was a small unit of manually set type, which was checked before being merged into a frame with other galleys. The galley proof—also called a *reader's proof*—was used to check for errors in manual typesetting.

gang run

Two or more printing jobs run simultaneously on the same press. Large sheets of paper are shared by several jobs and, after printing, are cut into sections corresponding to the separate jobs.

gloss ink

A quick-drying ink used on coated paper.

glue binding

A method of binding that depends on glue, also called *perfect* binding.

glyph

In electronic publishing a glyph is any character of a font. A glyph is normally a letter, number, or mark of punctuation. But it can also be a graphic symbol or a decorative element known as a dingbat.

goldenrod

Orange or yellow paper used as backing for material to be photographed by a process camera.

grain

In a sheet of paper, the direction in which most of the fibers lie. The grain is the easy-tearing or folding direction. It ordinarily parallels either the length or the width of the sheet.

grain long/grain short

If a paper's length parallels the grain, it is called grain long. If the paper's width parallels the grain, it is called grain short.

graphics arts camera

A camera used to film copy for printing. Also called a *process camera*.

gravure printing

An alternative both to relief printing and to lithography. Instead of being confined to the raised areas of the plate, or to the dry areas where it can adhere, the ink is held in the plate's tiny carved or etched recesses.

gray-component replacement (GCR)

A method for systematically replacing colored inks by black ink in areas where dots of all three colored inks are interspersed. It begins by eliminating equal amounts of each ink. The color that remains is lighter, because the combination that was eliminated would have contributed a neutral gray. The same neutral darkening can then be restored using black ink as a replacement. GCR saves ink and can improve the quality of an image.

greeking

Gibberish used to take the place of real text for layout purposes.

gripper edge

The gripper edge of a sheet of paper is the leading edge where the sheet is grasped mechanically and drawn into the press.

gripper margin

Unprinted space allowed along the gripper edge.

gutter

The inner margins where two pages meet.

gutter bleed

A synonym for *crossover*.

Glossary *(continued)*

hairline

The finest line that can be reproduced, thinner than half a point.

hairline registration

Registration accurate to within plus or minus half a row of dots.

halftone process

A method of resolving continuous-tone art into fields of dots. Darker areas in the original are represented by patches where the dots are larger (in the most common process), or closer together. Resolution into dots can be done digitally, by a process called *digital screening*, or it can be done photographically.

halftone screen

A grid used in the photographic halftone process to resolve continuous-tone copy into dots.

halo effect

Occurs when ink builds up at the edge of an area, making the interior look lighter.

hanging indent

A document style in which the first line of a paragraph is aligned with the left margin, and the remaining lines are all indented an equal amount. An effective style for displaying lists of information, sometimes referred to as outdenting.

head trim

The allowance for trim (usually 1/8-inch or 3mm) between the tops of pages.

headline

A short line of emphasized text introducing the body text that follows.

headline font

A font that has been designed for use in headlines. Headlines normally use a restricted set of characters, so headline fonts can contain fewer characters than other fonts.

hickey

A doughnut-shaped imperfection in presswork caused by dirt, paper particles, etc.

highlight

The lightest area in a photograph or other piece of continuous-tone copy.

hints

In electronic typography, hints are mathematical instructions incorporated into a digital font to improve its appearance at different resolutions.

image-editor

A computer program for editing raster image files and preparing images for publication. Among other functions, an editor can be used to crop, size, correct color balance, color-separate, and screen images for halftone reproduction.

imaging, imagesetting

A stage of publication in which digital document files are transferred to film, or some other medium, which will be used to produce plates for printing.

imposition

The arrangement of pages for printing on a large sheet in such a way that they appear in order when the sheet is folded.

impression cylinder

A cylinder that presses paper into contact with an inked surface.

indirect color process

Separation and screening done as separate photographic steps. Original continuous-tone color copy is separated into (typically) four continuous-tone negatives, which are screened into dots at a later stage. This is in contrast to the direct process, which does both separation and screening in one step.

ink coverage

A percentage indicating the inked area of the paper.

inkometer

A tool for measuring the tackiness or stickiness of ink. Also called *tackoscope*.

inner form

The part of an imposition that consists of inside pages. On a printed sheet, the inner form pages are those that will be on the inside when the sheet is folded into a signature.

intaglio

Carved or etched recesses in a plate. These recesses hold the ink in gravure printing. Also called *gravure*.

interpolation

A method of calculating intermediate values. Digital image-editing employs several different interpolation methods for determining the color levels at each pixel.

italic

A slanting or script-like version of a face. The upright faces are often referred to as roman.

jogging

Vibrating a stack of sheets before binding or trimming. Used to bring the edges into line.

justified

In typography, text is justified if it is flush on both the left and right margins. Text that is *flush-right* or *flush-left*, in other words aligned on only one margin, is sometimes described as being *right-justified* or *left-justified*.

kerning

The adjustment of horizontal space between individual characters in a line to create a perception of uniformity; critical where large typefaces are used, as in headlines.

keyboard layout, keyboard mapping

A keyboard layout or mapping is the table governing which character is generated when a particular key or combination of keys is pressed.

lacquer

A transparent, protective coating that gives a high gloss to printed paper.

Glossary *(continued)*

lap

A slight overlap of printed colors. It can be the result of trapping, a method used to allow for faults in registration.

laydown sequence

The order that colors are printed.

leading (pronounced: ledding)

The amount of space added between lines of text to make a document legible. The term originally referred to the thin lead spacers that printers used to separate lines of metal type. Leading can be adjusted where necessary to get extra lines of text on a page.

letterpress

Relief printing directly onto the paper. The oldest form of printing. Raised areas of the plate hold the ink and transfer it directly. This is in contrast to intaglio or gravure printing, where sunken recesses hold the ink, and also in contrast to offset printing, where the originally inked surface does not come in direct contact with the paper.

letterset

Offset letterpress printing. The image is defined by raised areas, as in the direct case. The raised areas get inked, but do not come in contact with the paper. Instead, the image is transferred to a blanket, which in turn transfers it to paper. Also called *dry offset*. Resembles offset lithography in using a blanket as intermediary.

letterspacing

Letterspacing adjustments are applied to a block of text as a whole, and are sometimes referred to as tracking or track kerning. This is distinct from ordinary kerning, which adjusts space between individual letters. Letterspacing is used to improve legibility and to fit more or less text into the given space.

ligature

Two or more letters taken as a unit. In some typefaces, certain pairs of letters overlap in unsightly ways if printed side by side. Substituting a ligature improves the appearance in these cases. Examples of how ligatures are accessed from the keyboard are: fi (Shift + Option + 5) and fl (Shift + Option + 6).

line copy, line art

Artwork that is black on white, or solid color on white, without middle tones. Photographic methods that eliminate middle tones for special effect are sometimes used to convert continuous-tone art to line art.

lithography

In lithography, wetness and dryness define the image. Dry areas on the plate pick up ink and transfer it. In the offset case the transfer to paper is indirect, via blanket. Dry area here plays a role analogous to raised area in letterpress, or sunken area in gravure. Commercial printing is mainly offset lithography.

makeready or set

The steps or time needed for preparing the press for a job. Makeready may include the preparation of folding and binding equipment.

margin

The white space around text blocks. Margins typically need to be created on the edges of a page, since most printers can't print right to the very edge. White space also makes a document better looking and easier to read.

metallic inks

Inks with a metallic sheen. A metallic ink consists of metal powder dispersed in a medium that binds it to the paper. Powdered bronze is used to make gold ink.

multilith

A small-format offset lithographic press. Can be used to print individual pages rather than multiple pages imposed on large sheets.

oblique

A slanting version of a face. Oblique is similar to italic, but without the script quality of a true italic.

offset

Printing that uses an intermediary surface called a blanket to transfer the image from the primary inked surface to the paper.

overprinting

Printing one color over another. In a design with overlapping colored areas, the upper-most area determines the levels of inks that are shared.

pagination

The page numbering in a book.

Pantone Matching System (PMS)

The registered trade name of a system of color matching, applied to inks, papers, and related design materials.

paragraph rules

Graphic lines that separate blocks of text and isolate graphics on a page. Some desktop applications provide for paragraph styles to be created that include paragraph rules.

paste up

Assembling camera-ready copy with adhesive. The result, typically a collage of text and line art, is sometimes called a *mechanical*.

perfect binding

An unsewn, flat-spined binding made with glue. Also called a *glue binding*.

perfecting press

A type of press that prints simultaneously both sides of the paper, as it passes between two cylinders.

Glossary *(continued)*

pi characters

Special typographic characters, such as mathematical symbols, not included in ordinary fonts.

pica

A unit of measure that is approximately one-sixth of an inch. A pica is equal to 12 points. The traditional British and American pica is 0.166 inch. In PostScript printers, a pica is exactly 1/6 inch.

piling

A printing problem in which ink pigment accumulates on a plate or blanket.

pinhole flaw

A type of flaw that occurs in film.

platen

A type of flat letterpress that uses a hinged clamping action to bring the paper and plate together. The platen is sometimes called a *clamshell* press.

point

A unit of measure in typography. Normally there are 72 points to the inch.

point size

The common way to describe the size of a font. A font's point size is the distance in points from the top of the highest ascender to the bottom of the lowest descender.

press proof

A proof pulled from the press prior to actual print run. Rarely done due to cost, but done in lieu of contact proof.

press run

The number of copies in one printing.

process camera

A camera specially designed for process work such as color separation, halftone screening, and producing film for plate making. Also called a *graphic arts camera* or *copy camera*.

progressive proofs or progs

Proofs made on a press. Each color is shown separately and various combinations are shown overprinted. Progs are used as a guide in adjusting the final color quality.

quad

A typesetting term for a specified space size. For example, an em quad is the size of a letter M and an en quad is the size of a letter N.

ragged right/ragged left

Unaligned at the right or left margin. *See* flush left ragged right.

raised cap

A design style in which the first capital letter of a paragraph is set in a large point size and aligned with the baseline of the first line of text. Compare to a drop cap.

raster image

An image recorded by specifying the color at each cell of a grid. An individual cell in the grid is called a pixel (short for "picture element") and the grid of pixels is called a raster. Digital scanners produce raster image files from flat copy, and image-editing software supports on-screen modification of images by processing raster image files.

reader's proof

See galley proof.

ream

Five hundred sheets of paper.

register

The correct alignment of colors during printing.

register mark

A cross-and-circle mark defining the correct alignment of overlay copy and color during printing.

relief plate

A printing plate with a raised, image-bearing surface. Letterpress uses a relief plate. Photoengraving, not to be confused with gravure, also uses a relief plate.

reverse type, reverse text

Type that is printed white on black, or light-colored against a dark background.

roman

The upright style of a typeface, as contrasted with its italic version.

rotary printing

Any method using a cylinder as the primary inked printing surface.

rotogravure

Gravure printing on a rotary, web-fed press.

rubber plate

A flexible relief plate used in flexography.

rule

A solid or dashed graphic line in documents used to separate the elements of a page.

saddle-stitching

A type of binding that uses wire stapling at the center of a magazine or pamphlet. Folded spreads are placed over a peaked frame called a saddle and stapled through the middle. A similar type of binding is also done with thread.

sans serif font

A typeface without serifs, generally a low-contrast design. Helvetica is an example.

scanner

A device for producing raster image files from flat copy—photographs, artwork, or text—by optical scanning.

Glossary *(continued)*

secondary color

Secondary colors are pairwise combinations of primaries. Seen under magnification, an inked area must either be one of the three primary colors, or one of the three secondary colors, or black. Halftone dots and the overlaps between them can only be of six colors, plus black. The sensation of full color on a page results from the additive mixing of these six colors.

selection tools

Essential features of image-editing software. These tools allow the designer to cordon off selected parts of a raster image and to designate particular objects for on-screen modification. Examples from Adobe Photoshop are the wand and lasso.

self-cover

Using the same paper for the cover and the inside pages.

serif

In typeface design, a small, decorative stroke appearing at the ends of the main strokes that define a letter. Horizontal serifs serve to lead the eye along a line of type.

sheet-fed press

A printing press into which individual sheets of paper are fed, as contrasted with a *web-fed* press printing on a continuous strip as it unrolls.

show-through

When the impression on one side of a sheet is visible on the other side, through the paper.

side-stitching

A method of binding that involves stapling through the spine of a publication from front to back. This prevents the book from lying flat, when it is opened to a page.

signature

A group of pages printed on the same sheet, front and back. After printing, the sheet is folded so that the pages fall in correct order.

skewing

When press cylinders are not parallel and do not make proper contact. Can also occur if pages are stripped crooked.

slurring

A printing problem in which halftone dots appear elongated or smeared.

spine

The backbone of a book, particularly of the binding.

splice

Join webs of paper, head to tail, so as to begin feeding from a fresh roll.

spoils, spoilage

Unsatisfactory sheets discarded before delivery.

spread

A pair of facing pages. Also called *two-page spread* or *double-truck*.

stet

A proofreading term meaning "let it stand": an instruction to ignore a proposed change and print as in the original.

strike-through

See show-through .

stripping

Assembling film into flats for plate making.

style

One of the variations, such as italic and bold, that comprise a typeface family.

SWOP

The acronym for Specifications Web Offset Publications. It refers to a booklet giving standards for web-fed offset printing.

symbol font

A font consisting primarily of mathematical symbols rather than ordinary letters and numbers.

tabular figures

Numerals that all have the same width. This makes it easier to set tables of data.

tack

Adhesive quality, or stickiness, of ink.

thermography

An embossed effect obtained by applying resinous powder to a wet image and fusing it with heat.

thinners

Liquids mixed with ink to reduce tack.

three-color process

The conventional four-color process omitting black.

tint

Tints of a screened color differ only in the size of the dots, not in the proportions of component primaries. They vary in tonal strength, but not in hue.

tissue overlay

A tissue flap attached to artwork as a protective cover.

tracking

The average space between characters in a block of text. Sometimes also referred to as letterspacing.

trapping

In color printing, any of several methods used to prevent visible gaps from appearing between two adjacent regions not bridged by a common ink. Such gaps can result from the occasional slight misalignment of different color impressions. Trapping often involves expanding the lighter of two adjoining regions so as to overlap with the darker

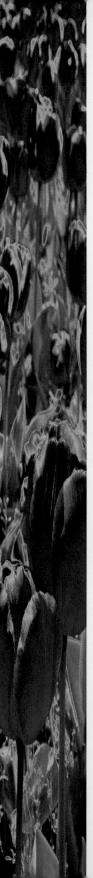

Glossary *(continued)*

trim marks

Marks indicating where to trim. Also called *cut marks*.

TrueType

A scalable type technology.

turnaround

The time from start to finish of a particular job.

Type 1

The international standard format for digital type, available on almost every computer platform. Originally invented by Adobe Systems, Type 1 is now the most commonly available digital type format and is used by professional digital graphic designers. More than 30,000 fonts are available in the Type 1 format.

typeface

A design for the letters, numbers, and symbols comprising a font, often part of a family of coordinated designs. Individual typefaces are usually identified by a family name and some additional terms indicating style, weight, and width.

typeface family

See font family.

typeface styles

Within a typeface familiy, variants such as roman, backslant, and italic.

typeface weights

Darkness variants within a single typeface family, including thin, light, bold, extra-bold and black.

typeface widths

Width variants within a single typeface family, including extended, condensed, and normal width.

typographic color

The darkness of a block of text. This depends on the thickness of the strokes that make up the characters, as well as the point size and leading used for setting the text block.

undercolor removal (UCR)

Removing the colored ink from areas where all three overlap, and replacing the dark overlap color with black ink. Eliminating redundant ink reduces cost and helps avoid problems connected with saturating the paper.

vector graphics

Digital images defined interactively on-screen, as a rule, using illustration software and the mouse. A vector image is determined by specified points and mathematical functions. Curves can either be generated automatically or drawn manually and approximated by series of line segments. Areas defined by curves may be filled in with color at the designer's choice.

watermark

A mark in paper that becomes visible when it is held up to the light.

web-fed press

A press printing continuously on a web, or roll, of paper.

wet-on-wet

Printing in which the first color of ink is still wet when the next is printed.

white space

The blank area on a page where text and illustrations are not printed; an important graphic element in page design.

widow

A single word or part of a word ending a paragraph of type. As a rule, the spacing between letters is adjusted to absorb such material into the main body of the paragraph.

word spacing

Adjusting the average distance between words to improve legibility or to fit a block of text into a given amount of space.

work-and-tumble

A type of sheet-fed printing in which front and back images share a single plate. The sheet is printed on one side, flipped head over heels, and printed on the other side. After flipping, the paper has a new leading edge, where it is gripped for handling, so allowances must be made for two gripper edges.

work-and-turn

Another type of sheet-fed printing in which front and back images share a single plate. The sheet is printed on one side and then turned right over left so that the back can be printed. This does not change the paper's leading edge, where it is gripped, so only one gripper edge is needed.

wrong-reading

A reversal of the original image or type, as if viewed in a mirror.

WYSIWYG

Pronounced "wizzy-wig," an acronym for "what you see is what you get." What you see on the computer screen corresponds to what you will get as printed output.

x-height

Traditionally, x-height is the height of the lowercase letter *x*. As a general rule, it is the height of the body of lowercase letters in a font, excluding the ascenders and descenders. Some lowercase letters may extend a little bit above or below the x-height as part of their design, even without ascenders and descenders. The x-height can vary considerably among typefaces with the same point size, which is based on the width of certain uppercase letters.

zinc engraving, zincs

Line or halftone art as relief etching on zinc plates for letterpress.

Index

Index *(continued)*

Index *(continued)*

Credits

Editor	*Leonard Cottrell*
Technical Editor	*Rita Amladi*
Cover and Book Design	*Andrew Faulkner and Lori Barra*
Production	*Eric and Jan Marti, Command Z*
Illustration	*Julie Brockmeyer*

Art & Photography

Adobe Image Library (pp. 7, 30-31, 74, 90-91, 97, 99, 100-105, 138, 162, 188, 196-197, 214, 216, 218, 220, 222, 224, 226, 228, 230)

Digital Stock Corp. (p. 67, Girl)

Amy Faulkner (pp. 10, 14, 54, 134, 170, 176-177, 178-179, 184-185)

Raymond Gendreau (pp. 7, 11, 15, 50, 55, 134, 139, 157, 166, 171, 182, 193)

Julieanne Kost (p. 65, Gourds; p. 95, Doorway, Ruins and Door Knockers)

PhotoDisc, Inc. (p. 107, 109, Tulips)

Karen Tenenbaum (p. 35, Coins; p. 111, Clock)

The Art of the Garden example is designed by Mario Mirilae of Mirilez Ross